The Humanist Ceremonies Handbook

FIRST EDITION

The Humanist Ceremonies Handbook

FIRST EDITION

*Writing and Performing Humanist Weddings, Memorials,
And Other Life-Cycle Ceremonies*

AUTUMN REINHARDT-SIMPSON

Humanist Press, LLC
Washington, DC

© 2018 Humanist Press, LLC
1821 Jefferson Place NW
Washington, DC 20036

www.humanistpress.com

Autumn Reinhardt-Simpson

The Humanist Ceremonies Handbook

Published by: Humanist Press, LLC

Cover Design: Lisa Zangerl

Cover Photo: © Iphotothailand | Dreamstime

Edited by: Rachael Berman, Humanist Society Celebrant Program Coordinator

Printed book ISBN: 978-0-931779-75-6

Ebook ISBN: 978-0-931779-76-3

Table of Contents

Preface

Over the years of my career as a humanist celebrant curious people have often asked me many questions. Why are you a celebrant? Why do humanist couples not just go to the courthouse? Why don't they just go to a Unitarian Universalist minister? What meaning could a humanist funeral or memorial service have if you don't believe in an afterlife? Why would humanist parents want a baby-naming and guideparents? Isn't all this just copying our traditionally religious friends? I find that the questioners often have a stereotype of humanists as cold and rational, our decisions and actions occurring in the realms of a colorless utilitarianism and benevolent self-interest, making ceremonies seem oddly out of place.

But as we know, humanist lives are full of meaning and important moments. We also know that no one truly makes a decision or judgment free of emotion. Humanists are not just a group of people who reject the supernatural - they are a group of people who find incredible meaning and love in the world around them, in everyday circumstances as well as in milestones. When a humanist approaches marriage, childbirth, or death, they feel the same fear, anticipation, and excitement as other people. When they approach these important life transitions, they, like anyone else, want to celebrate and share them within their communities.

Humanism is not just an absence of supernaturalism, it is an established philosophy and, for some, a "religion," with roots going back thousands of years and continuing to grow into the future. Due to its nature as an inquisitive philosophy, it has taken many different shapes over time but has always had one consistent theme - that human beings are meant to inquire fearlessly into their world and base their conclusions and actions on reason, compassion, and justice, having no respect for revealed truths of any kind. Humanism is not merely atheism or agnosticism but rather a philosophy of both thinking and doing, dedicated to the improvement of our world. Humanists desire like anyone else to express their philosophy and values through their ceremonies.

For this reason, a simple visit to the courthouse doesn't work for many who want a wedding or memorial reflective of who they are, what they value, and how they live.

This was the reason that in 1939 a group of nontheistic Quakers created the Humanist Society of Friends to provide trained leaders to help humanists celebrate their important rites of passage. The founders thought it was important that nontheists be allowed to celebrate life on their own terms instead of forcing them to make do with traditional religious representatives, some of whom did not share their convictions.[1] The society continues its mission today as the Humanist Society, an adjunct of the American Humanist Association, a religious nonprofit institution providing celebrant endorsement to nontheists of all stripes and all over the globe. This includes nontheistic religious people, atheists, agnostics, post-theists, humanists, naturalists, and everything in between.

Humanists, like anyone else, deserve the right to have their own ceremonies to mark life events. However, celebrants don't just read a standard ceremony and many celebrants find that the hardest job they have is in the details. I have written this book as a guide to new celebrants who are curious about all the details of celebrancy; everything from applying with the Humanist Society, to consulting with clients, writing a ceremony, directing the action, running a business, and knowing how to sign a marriage license. I have also made sure that this book can serve as a help to everyday humanists who wish to write their own ceremonies to be performed by others, as well as for those who may not identify as humanists but still wish to craft a ceremony with humanist or nontheistic elements. I have included much of my own experience as a former celebrant, chaplain, and member of the board of the Humanist Society. But I believe that this sort of resource is all the better for having a diversity of voices and it therefore includes the experiences of others, both official celebrants and those who, while not officially endorsed by the Humanist Society, provide a similar service to their own communities. It represents the thought and hard work of many people out there who believe that ceremonies are a powerful way of expressing their values and of living in community.

I would also like to mention the American Humanist Association Education Department, which provides excellent training programs for humanist celebrants. If you can take an AHA celebrant training course, do it! But if you're not ready to commit to that yet, and want to learn something about humanist celebrations, I offer this book as a strong start.

I would like to recognize the people who made this book so much more than my own opinions and experiences and therefore, made it better and more universal. Anne Barker, Unitarian Universalist minister at Westwood Unitarian Congregation in Edmonton, Alberta contributed some of the most moving and sensitive passages which you'll find throughout this book in her name; Joshua Lewis Berg; Ian Bushfield, Executive Director of the British Columbia Humanist Association and a staunch proponent of social justice in humanism; Jason Callahan, humanist chaplain at the Medical College of Virginia, part of Virginia Commonwealth University, generously shared his time and experiences with me on a very difficult day during which he had lost a colleague; Fred Edwords; Tiffany Green, celebrant, close friend, and constant giver of pep talks; Frank Harlan; Jone Johnson Lewis; Patrick McGraw; S.Collins; Keith Robinson; Roy Speckhardt for allowing me to run with my idea; D. G. Van Curen; and Jessica Xiao, formerly of Humanist Press, for her honesty, hard work, and bravery. Of course, I must thank my husband David for taking over toddler duty on the days I worked to meet deadlines for this book as well as my doctoral work. Thank you also to all the couples, photographers and celebrants who contributed original photos, ceremonies, and tips to this book, for which they are properly credited. Writing is a communal process and anything valuable in the finished product is because of your participation.

Autumn Reinhardt-Simpson

November, 2017

A Note on the Text: You might have noticed that some writers capitalize *humanism* and others don't. There are no rules about this but, generally speaking, those who capitalize it are often those who see humanism as their religious outlook. Many philosophical humanists tend to prefer the lower case. I have decided to stick with the lowercase spelling for ease in reading. The only exceptions are when using direct quotes or excerpting other works.

CHAPTER 1

What is Humanism?

Ask anyone to define humanism and you'll get a variety of answers, some even contradictory. For instance, some say that humanism is the same as atheism while others say it is a philosophy of its own that can incorporate atheism. Others see humanism primarily within the context of history and the humanities. Others see it from a political standpoint, as an outlook focused on utilitarianism and the betterment of human kind. While some will say that humanism necessitates abandoning religion, others have incorporated it into their religious outlook. With all this diversity, it's not surprising that many *humanists* are confused about humanism!

Humanism is a word that gets thrown around quite a bit and is often used inaccurately. The problem with humanism is that it describes many different schools of thought that have existed since ancient times. Before I settle on what humanism means for our context, we really need to explore what it has meant throughout time and to different communities. It's only then that we can see the unifying thread that holds the humanisms together. You may notice that many of these different types of humanism can overlap and that some humanists identify with more than one label.

Literary humanism is usually our first introduction to the concept of humanism. Literary humanism is the study of what is called the humanities - art, science, literature, etc. This is the kind of humanism that you often find in the academy. It can loosely be expressed as appreciation of the artistic, literary, and scientific output of human beings.

Renaissance humanism was developed during a time period in which there was a renewed confidence in a human being's ability to determine truth for themselves. This resulted in a flourishing of art, science and literature that reflected the search for truth and humankind's place within it. Literary humanism is thus closely connected to renaissance humanism.

Religious humanism is an integration of humanist ethical philosophy with traditional religion that has an emphasis on human needs. Religious humanists may be deists, post-theists, or non-theists but all usually find a good fit in religious communities. Examples include Christian atheists, religious naturalists, Ethical Culturists, and many Unitarian Universalists.

Christian humanism is the belief that freedom, conscience, and rational inquiry are compatible with Christianity rather than opposed to it. Christian humanism is a form of religious humanism that came about during the renaissance and the subsequent increased confidence in exploring theology from a human-centered perspective. Some Christian humanists are theists while others call themselves either post-theistic (in which the god question is a distraction) or Christian Atheists. Some notable Christian humanists are John Shelby Spong (recipient of the American Humanist Association's Religious Liberty Award in 2016), influential theologian Paul Tillich (1886-1965), and prominent Christian pastor Brian McLaren.

Modern humanism is a naturalistic philosophy relying on science and reason to guide humans in searching for truth. It is the main underpinning of both religious and secular humanism (see below).

Secular humanism embraces naturalism and scientific inquiry as the basis for understanding life while rejecting the supernatural and revealed dogma. Religious opponents often refer to secular humanism as a "religion" and claim that its primary goal is the eradication of religion in the world, especially the public sphere (a circular reasoning if ever I heard one). Most secular humanists would reject this claim.

Humanistic psychology is the study of what helps humans to succeed. While most psychology focuses on sickness and pathology, humanistic psychology is more concerned with studying the conditions in which humans can most readily flourish.

Philosophical humanism is an umbrella that can encompass all of the above. It is the philosophical and ethical stance emphasizing the value and agency of human beings.[2]

Photo will be included in May, 2018 edition

I want to offer a short word about an emerging use of the word "humanism" that is not related to the religious and/or philosophical use employed by the larger humanist movement and should not be confused with the most accepted definitions of the word. *Antifeminist "humanism"* is a reaction to the increasing inclusivity of humanism. There are many self-identified humanists who reject the idea that women are oppressed and, in fact, some that embrace the idea that we live in an era in which women are oppressing men. You may have heard the statement, "I'm not a feminist, I'm a humanist." This statement is used to mean that concentrating on the oppression of women is distracting to the ideal of creating a worldwide human family. Often, proponents of this idea have latched on to the word "human" in "humanism" as a universalizing concept without investigating the long tradition of social justice philosophy behind it. When the humanist undertakes a critical examination of the place of women in our world, objective evidence will show that women have indeed been oppressed for millennia and that such oppression is counter to our stated desire to create a better world for all. As Roy Speckhardt, executive director of the American Humanist Association, says, "Since egalitarianism is foundational to humanism, it's inherently a feminist philosophy."[3]

So Then, What IS Humanism?

Now that we've explored the many humanisms, it might feel even more confusing than when we started! All you have to remember is that humanism is an umbrella term that can include many different things.

In some forms, it can include traditionally religious people such as theists and it even gives its name to a branch of psychology. However, humanism as understood by the Humanist Society can best be described as modern humanism and is summed up using the definition given by its parent organization, the American Humanist Association:

> *Humanism is a progressive philosophy of life that, without theism and other supernatural beliefs, affirms our ability and responsibility to lead ethical lives of personal fulfillment that aspire to the greater good of humanity.*[4]

The above is a quotation from the Humanist Manifesto III, one part of a series of living documents that clearly describes our humanist values and our responsibility to each other and the world. It is extremely important that all potential celebrants be very familiar with this foundational document and its predecessors. I've included all three texts, as well as a short history of them in the appendices at the end of this book.

A Word About Religious and Secular Humanists:

As a celebrant, you will most likely be encountering mainly religious and secular humanists (along with the vaguely unchurched) so it is good to examine them in more detail:

The main difference between secular and religious humanists is not one of philosophy but rather of practice, or, as Fred Edwords says, "The only difference between religious and secular humanists is how they spend their weekends."[5]

Religious humanists view humanism as either their religion or a vital element of it, and often participate in churches, Ethical Culture Societies, and other traditionally structured groups, whereas secular humanists view humanism as a philosophy and may or may not participate in ritual or group structures. These two types of humanism, the religious and the secular, came together in the early twentieth century to form what we know now as modern humanism.

And honestly? That's all. Belief in broad humanist principles is the same. Further, not all religious humanists go to church. And some who fit the definition of religious humanists will prefer to identify with secular humanist causes for their own reasons. The important thing here is to realize that you are dealing with individuals who have many different reasons for identifying as humanists and you have to be prepared to leave your prejudices at home when working as a celebrant.

CHAPTER 2

Humanist Celebrants

Now that you know a little more about humanism, let's explore in more detail the role of a humanist celebrant.

A humanist celebrant as endorsed by the Humanist Society is a qualified representative of that society who is able to create and perform meaningful ceremonies that celebrate the important events in our lives. They are accorded the same rights and privileges granted by law to priests, ministers, and rabbis of traditional theistic religions. As a celebrant, you must be knowledgeable about humanism because you will field lots of questions! At almost every ceremony I have ever done, I was approached by at least one person who asked me what humanism and a humanist celebrant are. As a representative of the Humanist Society, it is vital to have an expansive knowledge of humanist philosophy and practice.

But there are situations when you don't have the time to sit down and have a long philosophical conversation about humanism, such as when talking to wedding guests at a crowded reception. It's just for this reason that you may want to prepare an "elevator speech" about humanism and what a celebrant does. An elevator speech is a very brief and clear explanation, one which you could deliver to someone within the time it takes to ride an elevator. The best way to create one is to use the "Who, What, When, Where, Why?" formula. Remember to use brief, clear, everyday language to answer the following questions:

Who are you?
(I'm Autumn, a humanist celebrant, endorsed by the Humanist Society.)

What exactly do you do?
(Create and officiate personalized, original ceremonies for fellow humanists or others who want a secular ceremony.)

When do you do this?
(Anytime someone wants to mark an occasion.)

Where does this take place?

(Anywhere, we don't have a church!)

Why do you do this?

(It's important that humanists have the option of ritual when expressing their values and beliefs.)

Using my simple answers above, I've created an elevator speech that sounds something like this:

"I'm a humanist celebrant, endorsed by the Humanist Society. Humanists are people with a common ethical philosophy, similar in some ways to traditional religious groups, but who don't believe in the supernatural, like theistic gods and miracles. We have our own communities and ceremonies that express our ethical values. I help by creating and officiating weddings, memorials, etc. Since we don't have churches, we can perform these anywhere and in any way that is important to us. I really love doing this work because some of us like having the option of meaningful ceremonies just like our traditionally religious friends."

Notice that because I am keeping this short and simple, I've had to leave out a lot of nuance, such as the fact that not all humanists like to gather in groups, or even what specifically humanism is. Don't worry! Remember that this is simply an introductory speech, something short that won't overwhelm your listener with philosophical details. It also leaves out any bad-mouthing of traditional religion, something that turns listeners off and shifts the focus from positive humanism. At the end of my little speech, I usually give the listener my card. That way, they can always check out my website for more information about humanism and what I do.

Make sure you practice your elevator speech every chance you get! Humanism and humanist celebrants will often be a new concept for your listeners and conversations can become awkward if you haven't fully thought through and articulated your role in advance. By practicing often, you will also get a better understanding of what you do, which will help you confront ethical and professional challenges.

Why the Word "Celebrant"?

Humanist celebrant is the official term chosen by the Humanist Society, after careful thought. Some people use officiant, minister, or other titles, thinking those terms are better understood by their audience. I am constantly referred to as a minister, even though I don't call myself one. However, "officiant" and "celebrant" are both unintelligible to some people who only understand my role as ministerial. For this reason, I call myself a humanist celebrant but answer to other titles. This is illustrated by my recent move to Canada, where people are unfamiliar with "celebrant." The more common usage here is "officiant." You are not legally bound by the Society to a particular title, but it will be better for everyone in the long run to promote more widespread acceptance of the "celebrant" brand. What is most important is to make your role understood.

Ethics

With all this freedom to create unique ceremonies, various ethical questions will come up regarding your role. I'm going to address these more specifically later in this book when I talk in more depth about doing specific ceremonies. Let's just say here that it pays to know where your personal and professional boundaries lie well in advance of doing your first ceremony. You might get a sense of what these are by visiting the Humanist Society Official Code of Conduct guidelines. Aside from whatever personal boundaries you want to impose on yourself, you will be bound by this code as an endorsed celebrant. I have reproduced it here by kind permission from the Humanist Society.[6]

Celebrant Code of Conduct

Represent Authentic Humanism

- A Humanist Celebrant shall uphold and represent the ethical and philosophical principles of humanism as expressed in Humanist Manifesto III: Humanism and Its Aspirations. A Humanist Celebrant shall not willfully distort or misrepresent humanism or the greater humanist community.
- The Celebrant may choose or not choose wording referencing divine/supernatural or otherwise non-humanist content. Just as priests may refer to scientific or humanistic ideals, so may we in-

clude spiritual ideas in our own ceremonies. However, this should only be to recognize the culture, traditions, or guests of the ceremony. It is unethical for a Humanist Celebrant to present as humanist prayer, scripture readings, or other explicitly supernatural elements or elements of other religions.

- A Humanist Celebrant shall adhere to and uphold the purposes, policies, and bylaws of the American Humanist Association and the Humanist Society; a Humanist Celebrant shall not willfully contravene or misrepresent the purposes, policies, and bylaws of the American Humanist Association or the Humanist Society.

- Celebrants should be honest in any interaction with the nature of humanism including scientific naturalism and human-based rational ethics. This is particularly important for ceremonies or coaching.

Maintain Humanist Values

- Celebrants should at all times conduct themselves in a manner that reflects the highest degree of honesty and integrity when dealing with clients.

- People and the diversity they represent should be valued. This includes diversity of belief. While Celebrants need not hide their own beliefs or avoid disagreements, Celebrants should reserve arguments for the proper time and place.

- A Humanist Celebrant shall be expected to treat others with courtesy, dignity, respect, and tolerance, and without prejudice or bigotry. Celebrants will treat those suffering from stress, trauma, or tragedy with the utmost empathy and care.

Maintain Professional Integrity

- Celebrants should treat any information divulged by clients with strict confidence at all times within the extent authorized by law.

- Celebrants should not use their position of respect to further any other paid or voluntary work.

- For official work, Celebrants should maintain a high standard of dress and reserve informal attire for times when such is called. "Vestments", if used, should be reserved and strictly humanist in nature.

- Celebrants shall protect the integrity of their profession by investigating and reporting violations that may occur.

- Celebrants should do business primarily as ambassadors of humanism. Financial compensation is appropriate for services provided, but profit-making should never override humanist values.
- In performing any service, Celebrants should never exceed their qualifications. This applies to the type and size of ceremonies, events or counseling. It is particularly important Celebrants provide no mental health services of any kind without proper qualifications.
- All Celebrants should be willing to act on behalf of those they are working with and provide referrals to more-qualified personnel whenever necessary, including psychologists, religious personnel, or other celebrants, as appropriate.
- A Humanist Celebrant shall be expected to work and interact with other Humanist Celebrants and Humanist Leaders In an atmosphere of collegiality, cooperation, and mutual benefit, and without undue enmity or disparagement.

Protect Those in Your Care

- Celebrants should not publicize the content of any ceremony or activity that has been completed without first ensuring that sufficient changes have been made to ensure that identification of the subject is impossible or that subjects have authorized, in writing, use of their likeness or ceremonies.

- Celebrants shall avoid exploiting those in their care especially for commercial, sexual, political, or other favors.

Harassment Policy

We strictly prohibit and will not tolerate harassment based on an individual's protected status, including but not limited to sexual or racial harassment. Humanist Celebrants are prohibited from harassing others. This conduct includes but is not limited to:

- Unwanted sexually suggestive statements, questions or jokes;
- Repeatedly rejected sexual flirtations, advances, or propositions;
- Pressuring for sexual activity, including offering employment benefits in exchange for sexual favors or denying employment benefits in response to a refusal to provide sexual favors;
- Offensive touching or assault, obscene gestures or suggestive sounds;

- Use of insults, slurs or negative stereotyping;
- Circulating individually targeted offensive jokes, pictures, or other similar material;
- Intimidating acts, such as bullying or threatening based on an individual's protected status;
- Falsely denying, lying about, or otherwise covering up or attempting to cover up conduct that is prohibited by this policy; or
- Any other conduct that shows hostility toward, disrespect for, or degradation of an individual based on an individual's protected status.

Violation of this harassment policy is grounds for immediate removal of endorsement.

Some celebrants impose on themselves a stricter code than the Society's. You might not be comfortable drinking a celebratory glass of wine with the couple or sticking around for the reception if invited. While you are bound by the Society's code of conduct, it is structured broadly to allow for variations of circumstance. You may be very close with your clients because of a past relationship and therefore, your interactions might be less formal, or maybe you feel that declining to take part in a toast would be rude. None of these approaches is wrong. So long as you abide by the official code of conduct, any further restrictions you decide on are up to you. For instance, I have met clients who subsequently became good friends of mine. My personal philosophy for these new friendships is that our relationship stays professional until after the ceremony and only then do we become friends. Only you can decide how your professional philosophy fits into the Humanist Society Code of Conduct. Please read it very carefully to make sure that you are always acting for the benefit of your clients and the Humanist Society. Besides, the code of conduct is not just a rule book - it keeps you out of trouble as well!

Professional/Personal Boundaries During Ceremonies

Besides general conduct toward clients, it is good to know beforehand where your boundaries lie as regards the ceremony itself. Though a celebrant performs what many call "secular" ceremonies, there are times when you might be asked to do interreligious wedding ceremonies, or to lead a funeral in which a family member asks to read a passage from the Bible. My approach (which may not be your approach) is that I have no problem performing ceremonies with theistic elements so long as it is clear that I will not lead that particular moment. For instance, I will not read a Bible verse but am happy to introduce a family member to do so. In fact, this can be a great opportunity to include a client's family in the ceremony, as Kenna Covington, a celebrant in North Carolina, discovered. Before marrying a couple one weekend, the grandmother of the bride approached her with a Bible in hand and asked her to read a passage during the ceremony. The Bible had belonged to her dead husband and was very important to her. Kenna very graciously and tactfully told her that it would have so much more meaning coming from the grandmother herself because she could also tell the assembly about her husband who was not alive to share this special day. The grandmother agreed and the result was a touching and very meaningful addition to the wedding ceremony.

There are, in fact, many culturally religious humanists who may want to have religious rituals or elements as part of their ceremony, even if they are not practicing themselves. I once did a wedding for a Jewish couple who were atheist/humanist. Their Jewish heritage was very important to them and they wanted to have traditional Jewish elements included in their wedding ceremony. I made everyone happy by encouraging family members to get involved and say the traditional prayers. This was well inside my comfort zone because I was not being disingenuous and also allowed family and friends to be true to their heritage and beliefs. In cases such as these, it is very important to decide far beforehand what you are comfortable with and to make sure that clients are aware of this as well. It will save you lots of headaches!

Vital Points of Ethics

Two of the most important ethical/legal items I mention to new celebrants are the following:

A celebrant is NOT a counselor. If you do not actually have the necessary education, training and qualifications of a counselor, you must refrain from counseling. It would be unethical to engage in it. A celebrant is also not a humanist evangelist. A celebrant's role is not to push their idea of humanism upon a client or the guests of any ceremony but merely to represent it to the best of their ability.

You will most often be called on to perform marriages, though there are countless other ceremonies you can create or lead. These include memorials, invocations, baby namings, etc. Weddings are the only ceremonies with legal obligations and therefore it is very important to know the laws and customs of your region before you begin doing any wedding ceremonies. Again, this will save you from surprises further down the road.

Qualities of a Celebrant

Are you celebrant material? In being endorsed as a celebrant, you are being acknowledged as a person who understands humanism well, is prepared to work with many different kinds of individuals, and is, above all, able to represent the body that certifies you. Remember that in becoming a celebrant, you are not just Autumn Reinhardt-Simpson, specific humanist with specific opinions and prejudices regarding humanism, religion, etc. You are agreeing to represent the Humanist Society and in doing so, should be as professional and inclusive as ethically possible when acting in that capacity. Bottom line – it's not all about you.

Besides professionalism and a knowledge of humanism, there are other things to think about when considering becoming a celebrant. Consider the following questions as you think about whether you're celebrant material!

Are You Ready to Be a Celebrant?

1. How much do you know about humanism?
2. Can you explain what you think/believe in an "elevator speech"?
3. Have you ever led a ceremony or program before?
4. Do you enjoy public speaking?
5. Do you have a strong speaking voice?
6. Are you organized enough to keep good records?
7. Can you stick to a deadline?
8. Do you belong to a humanist group or organization?
9. Do you have good writing skills?

Don't worry if you've answered "no" to any of the questions above (or "not much" to number one). All of these are areas you can begin to improve right away. Let's talk about this.

How Much Do You Know About Humanism?

If you answered "nothing" or anything similar to that, don't worry. Many humanists don't actually know enough about humanism to really articulate it well but you can start your learning today. There are tons of resources out there, but try these websites for a start:

- The American Humanist Association website has a ton of information about humanism as well as current events. This is a great first place to start. And if you're not already a member, join now. You will need to be a current member to apply for endorsement through the Humanist Society. http://americanhumanist.org/

- Humanists UK (formerly the British Humanist Association) is an absolute treasure trove of all things humanist. They have an education page on their site that serves as both a hub for educators as well as for those looking for more information about humanism. Bonus – the BHA has some amazing celebrants on board who have done some truly fantastic ceremonies. Make friends here! https://humanism.org.uk/

- Kochhar Online Humanist Education is available via the American Humanist Association Education Department. They provide both free and paid courses in humanist subjects and even in performing various ceremonies. You can also take online classes in humanist philosophy, activism, social justice and more. The institute also provides in-person celebrant trainings around the country. Check their website to see if there is one near you. http://cohe.humanistinstitute.org/

- The International Humanist and Ethical Union is "the global representative body of the humanist movement,"[7] and an NGO that works to affect policy internationally. Their site has an incredible amount of information about what's going on with humanism worldwide. http://iheu.org/

There is so much information out there on humanism, ethics, naturalism, religious humanism, ethical culture, and all other aspects of humanism. You can find even more links as well as book recommendations in the appendices of this book.

Can you explain what you think/believe in an "elevator speech"?

Have you ever tried to explain to someone what humanism is and what you think about it? If you're like many of us, you might have had a hard time explaining the specifics of what you believe. That's where your elevator speech comes in. Even if you have no idea where to start, spend a few minutes rereading the section on elevator speeches, write one, then PRACTICE!

Humanist celebrant Dave Spencer looks quite comfortable speaking in front of a large group! One thing Dave does well is remembering to look up from his text often to make eye contact.

Have you ever led a ceremony or program before?

Of course, you'll be a little ahead of the game if you've already offici-ated a wedding or led a church or club program, but even if you haven't, you're not alone. Many who apply to become humanist celebrants have not yet had a chance to officiate. The best thing you can do is to make yourself available to lead events and programs in any clubs in which you're a member. Another great idea is to contact an already endorsed celebrant and ask to tag along during some of their ceremonies. It might feel weird to ask this but I was honored to serve as a temporary mentor for a few people new to the field and most clients did not mind it at all.

Do you enjoy public speaking?

I'm afraid this one is nonnegotiable! If you don't like speaking in front of large groups, you might have a tough time as a celebrant. However, I really think that the problem here is one of fear and not one of innate ability. Most people with little speaking experience don't enjoy speaking in large groups because they're terrified! But the truth is that once you begin to understand the principles and start practicing, you'll see that it is actually fun. The best way to begin learning how to speak in large gatherings is to just jump in. If you think you need something more formal, considering joining your local Toastmasters group. Toastmasters International is an amazing leadership group that focuses on speaking and presentation skills. You'll get a lot of professional feedback by hanging out with these folks and you're almost guaranteed to find one in any city or town. https://www.toastmasters.org/

Do you have a strong speaking voice?

A celebrant should have a strong speaking voice. Though you may sometimes be given a microphone, this is not always the case and I had at least one wedding where the sound failed completely! Being both prepared for disaster and used to public speaking made overcoming this obstacle no big deal.

Even if you have the softest, most timid voice, you can still learn to cultivate a strong public speaking voice. As a former theatre nerd, I can tell you with some authority that the secret is in learning where in your body to speak *from*. What I mean by that is this - take a moment to notice how you're breathing right now. Is it a deep breath? A shallow one? Is it fast, unsteady, or does it feel like you've not really filled up your lungs? When we speak to our friends and family, we tend to speak using a shallow breath which is just fine. Our friends and family are usually nearby, they can hear us just fine so we don't need to worry about where our breath is coming from as we speak to them.

37

But now let's take a deep breath. Breathe in as much air as you possibly can, focus on filling the entire lungs, all the way to the bottom. Notice that when you do this, your abdomen pops out a bit. This is your diaphragm (the sheet of muscles separating the thoracic cavity from the abdominal cavity) expanding. When you breathe this way, you're ready to project your voice and projection is what makes you audible and clear to large groups. In short, you've put yourself in control of your breath and the muscles that are important to controlling it. You can practice voice projection using online videos. Just check YouTube for "voice projection" and you'll be well on your way to a confident and clear speaking voice.

Having a loud and clear speaking voice is only one aspect of having good speaking skills. You must also be able to enunciate your words. Just as texting your friend is much different in style from writing a wedding ceremony, your public speaking voice must be much more clear and intelligible than when casually chatting with a friend. For example, you will want to make sure you clearly speak each syllable of a word, rather than run them together as you would in friendly conversation.

Just for starters, try saying "February." Most people will pronounce this "Feb-yoo-ary" when in fact, there's an r in there! Though it sounds silly to harp on this one detail, you'll notice that correct pronunciation of words while projecting your voice makes sense and doesn't sound silly at all. In fact, it makes you easier to understand in large groups. It has the added benefit of making you sound confident and articulate.

I once saw a news anchor from our local TV station out in public after he'd finished up his shift. He hadn't bothered to remove his thick stage makeup and up close it was pretty ridiculous looking. However, on television this kind of makeup is necessary if the audience is to see the news anchors clearly. You don't notice the makeup from your living room and the same is true of correct pronunciation while speaking publicly. While you might feel a little funny enunciating so much, be assured that all your audience can hear are clear, articulate words.

Are you organized enough to keep good records?

If you answered no to this question, I suggest you pay lots of attention to acquiring this skill. Being organized is important for so many reasons, but most importantly because you will be performing legally binding ceremonies and must be able to recall any records that the state or client may ask for, including tax records. Aside from that, being organized is a necessity for anyone working with clients of any kind. I'll talk more about organization and record keeping in Chapter 6.

Can you stick to a deadline?

As a celebrant, you're not just performing the ceremony but also writing it. Add to that meetings with clients and proofreading your work, rewriting, etc. This means that you need to be diligent about sticking to timelines. After all, you can't just postpone a client's wedding ceremony!

I have several tricks for sticking to deadlines which I'll talk more about in Chapter 6. But a quick tip here is to put your clients' ceremony into your calendar as soon as you receive the deposit. Once you've done that, add other dates into your calendar for when you want to have drafts ready, etc. Stick as closely as possible to your self-imposed deadlines and you'll find that you'll have a much easier time.

Do you belong to a humanist group or organization?

This is a question that the Humanist Society will ask you on your application and, if at all possible, the answer should be yes. If you are performing ceremonies for a community, it is best to be a part of it.

Moreover, having a humanist community will help you to grow in your understanding of the philosophy. There aren't humanist organizations in every city or town, but that shouldn't stop you from applying. Remember, you always have the option of starting one yourself! When I moved to Canada in the summer of 2015, there were lots of humanists around but no humanist community. Community is very important to me so I decided that rather than lament the lack of a formal group, I should just start one myself and the Edmonton Ethical Culture Circle was born. It's been a great experience and I've met lots of great people. Moreover, my community provides me with a chance to act as a celebrant for them when the need arises.

Do you have good writing skills?

This is an incredibly important skill for a celebrant. No matter how amazing a speaker you are, if you can't write well, your ceremony won't come off as professionally as you'd like.

Something to remember is that writing a ceremony which will be spoken aloud is much different from writing prose that is meant to stay on the page. Though it may seem counter to an event like an emotional wedding, my advice is to use clear and simple language rather than complicated or flowery phrases. This helps everyone feel a part of the event. This doesn't mean you can't get creative but most guests (and indeed, the couple) aren't going to remember your complicated oration. What will stick in people's minds is elegance, simplicity, and sincerity. However, you also want to take the couple into account. You need to represent their style in your ceremony as well. A very casual and humorous couple may want something light and other couples may want something more formal and traditional. When I married some close friends of mine, I knew I was in for a ride. Both were fervent devotees of certain classic television shows that gave plenty of scope for jokes. They wanted lots of memorable TV quotes interwoven with my own writing and I was even asked to work in a surprise story about the groom's most embarrassing moment. (Alas, I was not able to pull off that part of the ceremony without tears rolling down my face no matter how hard I practiced.)

Though I had a great time writing and performing this ceremony, there is no ceremony that works for everyone. It is best to discover the mood and personality of the couple during the initial consultation. My favorite tactic is to ask about the overall ceremony. Do they want it to be formal, traditional? Or are they looking for more of a big party with lots of humor, jesting and raw emotion? It may take a while to tease these details out but getting an initial sense of what a couple is looking for will help you to plan your tone.

As I said before, you're not just the facilitator of a ceremony but its author (or co-author if you're writing it along with clients). Clients will be counting on you to have written something unique and meaningful for them. Though you don't need to be a best-selling author to do this, having some degree of writing skill is a must. If you're worried about your ability to write several different ceremonies a year, the only answer is to practice! Writing, like speaking publicly, only gets better the more you do it. As an author, it's important to me to write every single day, even if all I get out are a few hundred words. You don't have to write ceremonies to start working on your writing in general. Try doing a ten or fifteen minute free write each day. You'll soon see that your ability to form thoughts into words will be improved.

Other Qualities

Besides speaking and writing, you want to be able to look the part of a professional. This means understanding how to dress for the occasion. This was especially difficult for me during the wedding season of 2014 since by then I was enormously pregnant. Nonetheless, I managed to find suitable clothing. My rule was always this: to look as professional but unobtrusive as possible. For me, this often meant a black or gray dress with matching shoes and occasionally a scarf. (Pants for women are, of course, totally fine. I just couldn't get my giant pregnant belly into them!) Though I was going to a wedding, my job was not to be the focus but rather the facilitator, much like a stagehand in a play. Remember that in the case of a wedding you will be standing up front with the couple and all eyes will be drawn that way. You want your guests to focus on the happy couple and not on you and your amazing new fuchsia pantsuit.

Some couples may request that you wear something specific. This is entirely a matter of personal preference whether you choose to accept that condition. At times when I sensed that color scheme was a big deal for a couple, I tactfully asked them if there were any colors I should not wear. This was my own choice so that I, again, would not be standing out from everyone else and the focus could remain where it should be.

Another option is a stole. Some celebrants may not wish to wear one because of its association with traditional clergy but others find it use-

Some people just like to keep it casual. Remember to find out from your clients what mood they're going for. This will help you choose the right tone in which to write the ceremony as well as your attire.

ful in quietly announcing who they are to the assembly. Believe it or not, you can often purchase a humanist themed stole on Etsy! Another option is to wear a Happy Humanist necklace or lapel pin. You can find these types of accessories on sites such as Dyeingarts or EvolveFish. You should check your national and regional humanist associations as well since many sell accessories and we all like to support our local humanist organizations, right? http://www.dyeingarts.com/kit-humanist.html; http://www.evolvefish.com/

Humanist celebrant Charlene Komar Storey sports a colorful stole with the Happy Humanist visible on her right shoulder. She's capped it all off by wearing a silver humanist pendant.

CHAPTER 3

Humanist Wedding Ceremonies

Now that you know a bit more about humanism and you've assessed your celebrant qualities, it's time to talk ceremonies - the what and how. In this chapter, I'm going to take you through the traditional elements of a western wedding ceremony. We'll look at their different components, how to fit them together and, ultimately, tips on writing the ceremony itself. Of course, you don't have to limit yourself or your clients to a western format. However, it's a good place to begin exploring the ins and outs of crafting the one ceremony you will no doubt be asked to do more than any other.

Humanist Weddings

Many more people than ever are looking for nonreligious wedding ceremonies. While currently there are no available statistics for

*Many interreligious couples choose humanist celebrants
who can offer them either a nonreligious ceremony or one
that incorporates elements from both individuals' traditions.*

how many US weddings are specifically humanist, anecdotal evidence shows that at least secular, if not humanist, weddings are on the rise. This is especially true of second marriages and marriages among what is termed "millennials." This is no doubt partly because of an upswing in non-traditional religions as well as atheism and interfaith relationships. Moreover, many find the rigid structure of a traditional ceremony ill-suited to their personalities.

There is no such thing as a typical humanist wedding ceremony and therefore the biggest asset of the humanist celebrant is their ability to craft a completely unique event, tailored to the clients' needs and values. Another advantage of a humanist wedding is that it takes the focus off of a deity and puts it where it belongs: directly on the couple being celebrated. This is a great opportunity to create a ceremony that reflects the culture, values, and traditions of the couple themselves. The best part for me are the vows. They are made to each other as they should be and not to a god or church.

Your role as a celebrant is to create, facilitate, and conduct a meaningful and personalized ceremony that reflects the clients' values, hopes and dreams. This is not a time to proselytize or argue with a client's family over religion. In short, it is not about you! But it's a long journey to get to the finished product and it begins with the initial consultation.

Ian Sidden and Rebekah Westrum loved every minute of their personalized, meaningful humanist wedding ceremony.

Consultation

The consultation is always my favorite part aside from performing the wedding itself. This is your chance to analyze the situation and draw out your clients. I like to start by asking the couple to tell me how they met. This is a good strategy to see how the couple interacts with each other and to get a sense of their individual personalities. It also tends to put people at ease. Next, I ask them the most important question of all - why me?

Not everyone will have an answer as to why they chose you to celebrate their wedding. Some will say, "I'm a humanist and I want a humanist wedding!" But honestly, such people will be much fewer than those who say, "I just don't want a religious wedding." While it is true that we perform just such a service, it doesn't ensure that we are always the best match for them. I love asking clients why they want a humanist wedding because it gives me a chance to see if they have any idea what humanism is! While I have never required a "purity test" from my clients, I have had plenty of misunderstandings arise from potential clients who assumed I was traditionally religious. For example, I received a voicemail one day from someone asking if I could take over for a sick pastor at a wedding to be held at a Baptist church. It was clear that the caller found me in a directory of marriage officiants and assumed I was theistically religious in some way. I called the client back and left a message that I was certainly happy to do the wedding but also explaining that as a humanist, I would not myself perform a theistically-focused wedding. Needless to say, my return message went unanswered. Asking a couple why they chose me is not so much a test of their "worthiness" to be married by me but rather a good and tactful way to avoid future misunderstandings.

During the initial consultation (which I always provide free of charge and can be done in person or via Skype), I spend a lot of time drawing out details from the couple. I start with the very basics. What sort of feel do they want for the wedding? Formal? Informal? Do they want to involve family or friends? How many guests will there be? Do they have a venue yet? Are there any special elements such as rituals or important readings that the couple wishes to include? Will the ceremony include languages other than English and will translators or foreign language transcripts be needed? You don't have to ask a ton of questions and the clients do not yet need to have definite answers. This is very preliminary and clients always have more to add as you work through the process over the months leading up to the wedding. I always reassure my clients that they do not need to know what they want just yet. The details often come to them as we work through building the ceremony together. You may want to create a quick worksheet of standard questions to help you during the consultation process. Take a look at the breakout box below for inspiration.

James and Andrew met with Celebrant Donna Forsythe on several occasions and discussed everything they were looking for on their special day.

Consultation Questions

Reverend Anne Barker, Unitarian Universalist Minister, Edmonton, Alberta

"I ask both partners to individually answer each question, not necessarily in this order. (I rarely ask all of these questions, as new ones tend to pop up in response to the answers, and every couple is different. I don't give them the questions to look at because of this.)"

- How did you meet? (Or tell me your story....)
- What do you love about the other person?
- How do you spend your time together? What do you like to do?
- Why are you choosing to get married (or have a service of union) rather than simply living together?
- What are you promising to one another? ("Given our ever-changing cultural contexts, I don't make assumptions about

couples' promises to each other – and I make that clear to them, early on. I don't use language like 'fidelity', 'exclusiveness', 'forsaking all others', 'forever', 'lifetime promise' or "children' unless the couple tells me this is what they are planning or promising.")

- What is your philosophical / religious / spiritual history – as it informs this celebration? Is there any family component or tradition that needs to be incorporated?
- What do you imagine will be different after you are married?
- Tell me about your rings. What do they represent to you?
- What are you wearing for the wedding?
- The people who are attending – tell me what they mean to you?
- What do you hope your guests take away from the celebration? How would you like them to describe it?
- Is there anything else you really want included in this celebration?
- Is there anything you really don't want to happen during this ceremony?

Photo will be included in May, 2018 edition

Kenna Covington of North Carolina Secular Weddings also has a great worksheet she gives to her couples. Check it out and see if it gives you some ideas!

About the ceremony:

- Is there anything you definitely do or do not want to include in your ceremony?
- How comfortable are you with public speaking?
- Are there any traditions you would like to incorporate into your ceremony?
- Describe your guests and family - are they rambunctious, reserved?
- How formal will your wedding be - do you want the wording to be relaxed or formal?
- Will you be taking photos before or after the wedding?
- Is there any family/historical/cultural significance to your rings?
- How surprised with your ceremony do you want to be? I feel most comfortable creating the ceremony with you, but some people would rather be surprised.

About the wedding couple:

- How did you meet?
- When did you know you had fallen in love?
- Who and how did you propose?
- Describe your relationship in a few sentences.
- What do you think the key for you to live a long and happy life together will be?
- What do you like about each other?
- Do you have any marriage role models?
- Is there one overwhelming idea or concept you would like your guests to take with them - other than you love each other and you just got married?

The consultation is also a good time to have them look at sample ceremonies. It pays to have a few templates to work from when called on to do impromptu ceremonies and they can serve double duty as examples for your clients. It is also good to go through your contract and expectations at this point and to send them away with a copy of the contract and a reservation form with information about deposits (more on the business side of celebrancy in chapter 6).

The Relationship Story

Many celebrants, once they receive a deposit, like to give the happy couple a little homework. One of my favorite tactics for understanding a couple and thus, creating a tailored ceremony, is the relationship story. The relationship story is probably the most used tool by celebrants everywhere. I tell the couple to either together or separately write the story of their relationship in at least five hundred words. One couple I married had lots of fun with this assignment and wrote little comments and interjections in each other's stories using different colored font. It was playful and gave me enormous insight into how they interacted. I also ask each person secretly to tell me what the other means to them. It is always fun to surprise the couple with these quotes about each other during the ceremony. There is never a dry eye!

There are a lot of components to conducting your initial consultation but the most important part is to assure the clients that you have their interests at heart. Many couples are afraid that I might let a father or mother-in-law give me my orders. It is very important to let the couple know that you are doing a wedding for them and that you will do nothing, add nothing, take nothing away, without their first approaching you about it. I had a mother of a groom insist on changing several details on the day of the wedding. It was difficult but necessary to remain both professional and firm while explaining to her that I worked for the couple. She continued to ask me to change several things until I turned to the bride and asked, "What would you most like to do?" She later told me that that my directly asking her was the only way she found the courage to not give in to her mother-in-law!

I am a librarian and one thing we always say regarding reference librarianship is that your patron doesn't really know what information they're asking for until you draw it out of them. This is probably going to be true for most of your clients as well! They often know one, maybe two things by the time you have your initial consultation - they want to get married and they want it to be nonreligious. At that point, they're looking to you to draw out all the necessary details. Remember to reassure them that will happen over the next few weeks or months as you work together to craft a memorable experience!

Elements of a Traditional Wedding Ceremony

A traditional wedding has the following elements:

- The processional
- Opening words
- "Giving away" a bride (we'll talk about why this is a bad idea)
- Vows/Exchange of rings
- The pronouncement
- The recessional

Of course, this is just the traditional setup. Your clients may decide that this isn't the right formula for them and there are plenty of good examples of unorthodox weddings out there, some of which I've included in this chapter. However, I am going to assume that for most of you, this is the first ceremony you've ever written and, to walk you through it, we're going to use a traditional outline. After you've gotten the hang of it I encourage you to experiment with writing all sorts of different kinds of wedding ceremonies. After all, you're going to have a diversity of clients and you'll likely need a little of everything on hand.

Writing the Ceremony

The best way to tackle any writing assignment is to focus on one component at a time. Don't worry about how you're going to end a piece if you're just writing the opening words. Another thing to remember is that you can always go back and change parts of the ceremony. In other words, don't get stuck writing and rewriting the vows. Get the bare bones down and move on, no matter how awful they sound at first. Editing and rewriting are so much easier after you have a rough draft, no matter how rough. With that sage advice out of the way, let's get a bird's eye view of the general structure of a wedding ceremony.

A good way to visualize the structure of your entire ceremony is to imagine it as an hourglass. You want your opening to be broad and inclusive of family and friends as you welcome everyone to the ceremony. You might then use tidbits from the relationship story to set the scene, perhaps by telling how the couple met, etc. All of this gradually moves into sharper focus on the couple (the vows, exchange of rings, etc. are the narrow part of your hourglass) and then gradually move back out to a more general focus on the couple as part of a larger community.

Another way to think of it is that the top (broad) part of the hourglass is where you focus on the couple as two individuals coming from different places. You gradually narrow your focus (the middle of the hourglass) to the individuals uniting through vows and the exchange of rings. And finally, you begin to slowly broaden out again, focusing on the couple as a new unit within their community. To bring the focus back out to the community, you might say a few words about the responsibilities of marriage to the couple, as well as invite their community to support them. Or you might express your wishes to the couple. The idea is that you will be addressing them as a unit now and getting ready to send them into their community as such. You'll see this in more context below and in some of the examples at the end of this chapter.

So now that you have the basic outline, let's get writing!

The Processional

The processional is when the wedding party enters the venue, sometimes accompanied by grandparents or other family members, and takes their place at the front of the room. Some clients may wish for a very traditional processional while others might not care that a groom should supposedly stand on a specific side, etc. Whatever type of procession the couple settles on, guests generally like to stand up as a bride enters. If this happens, just remember that you need to ask them to sit down again once she's reached the front of the room, otherwise they'll stand there all day. Ask me how I know this.

Humanist celebrant Jessica Dapson leads the processional.

"Giving Away" the Bride

Usually the next step is to give away the bride but I advise strongly against including this element in any humanist ceremony because of its history as a symbol of ownership, something that is very antithetical to humanism. I personally refuse to do weddings in which the woman must be passed from her father's control to her husband's as it is incompatible with humanist philosophy as well as my own dignity as a woman. Though many don't realize it today, this practice originates from a time when western women had absolutely no legal independent existence except occasionally in widowhood. When a woman passed from her father to her husband, she entered a state of "civil death"; she was literally dead to the law.8 That is why she would henceforward be known as Mrs. John Smith and not a person with her own legal existence and name. As a woman and a feminist, this goes far beyond my comfort zone and I refuse to participate in it. You'll find that most women today don't want this in their ceremony either! When doing weddings, which have sometimes traditionally been a ritual of transfer of ownership, it is a good time to reflect on how your humanist values intersect with the rights and dignity of women. One way to turn this ritual on its head is to invite the parents of both clients to give their children away as a sign of transition and family blending. However, it is good to only do this if both clients' parents participate. If only a bride's parents take part, it becomes exactly what we were trying to avoid - a transfer of ownership.

Stephanie and Kimberly Allen and their daughter were all smiles throughout the entire humanist wedding ceremony.

Speaking of Gender Issues ...

So many amazing things are happening in our society right now, particularly with respect to the LGTBQ community. Marriage equality is a thing! People can now tick off "other" on questionnaires about gender! This is all amazing stuff and means that more people now than ever before can feel accepted on their own terms.

Sometimes, all these changes, though great, can become confusing, and pronouns can be the most confusing of all! It might be really hard to tell what someone's preferred pronouns are, especially when they present in a way that doesn't seem traditionally feminine or masculine (though keep in mind that some traditionally presenting people as well as straight, non-trans people still might prefer a different pronoun than you expect). A few years ago, I found myself really anxious about these kinds of situations because I thought it might be rude to just straight out ask. My friend, humanist celebrant S. B. Collins, who prefers "they" as their pronoun, set me straight. It's not only not rude to ask but very welcome! Asking someone what pronouns they prefer shows that you respect their autonomy and their ability to self-describe.

Whatever pronouns people choose, make sure you try to use them consistently both in the ceremony and in consultation. Most gender nonconforming people will forgive a few honest mistakes as you get used to them, but never purposely deny them their own personhood by using the wrong pronouns. This isn't about you. Make an honest effort to address everyone the way they prefer being addressed.

Charlene Komar Storey celebrates the marriage of two very happy women soon after marriage equality became law.

Pro Tip

"Always learn to pronounce people's names if you are not absolutely sure how to say it. When I have trouble remembering how to pronounce a person's name I will ask—often more than once, then write it phonetically at the top of each page of the script. Saying someone's name wrong over and over again during the wedding ceremony will negate all the work you may have put into it and is probably the number one least forgivable thing a celebrant can do. Only second to arriving late. Never do that."

— Frank Harlan, humanist celebrant,
Seattle, Washington

The Opening Words

Remember the hourglass structure? Your opening words are at the top of the hourglass along with the welcome. This is the part that is broadest which means your focus should be broad as well. You'll want to welcome the community, introduce the couple and say why you're there. You are essentially bringing everyone together for the occasion while setting the tone for the rest of the ceremony. A good example might be something like what I wrote for a gay couple who were only legally able to marry in 2015:

"On behalf of Tom and Mike, I want to welcome all of you, family and friends, who have come here today to celebrate something that should have taken place long before now. Your presence is evidence of your love and support for their union. Today is also a culmination of this community's efforts to not only support the love between these two men, but to ensure that such a union is recognized by society. Today we celebrate love, humanity, and progress."

Celebrant Joshua Berg delivers the opening words.

These opening words stay broad and expansive. They welcome everyone, imply the guests' roles as supporters of the future marriage, and state their importance to the couple. Further, for this couple and their friends and family, the fight for gay rights was bound up in their story of love, and it was important to them all to commemorate not just the marriage, but the context in which it was taking place - the legalization of gay marriage in Virginia.

After I've welcomed everyone and stated my purpose in calling them together, I like to say a few words about the importance of relationships and also tell a few stories about the couple as a way of beginning to narrow the hourglass toward a total focus on the couple and the most exciting parts of the ceremony - the vows and exchange of rings. This is where the relationship story comes in handy. If your couples did their homework well, you'll have plenty of good anecdotes to work with. A good structure is to start by telling how they met, funny stories about their time together, etc. and then bring it to a close with their personal words of love that you have separately collected from both of them.

The ring exchange can be both emotional and exciting!

This helps to wind down the hilarity of any anecdotes and begins to focus the audience on the two people in front of them.

The Vows, Exchange of Rings

Now that you've brought everyone in the room to tears and they're feeling all mushy, it's time for the vows and exchange of rings. This is also the part where you will ask if the couple consents to the marriage. THIS IS VERY IMPORTANT! In some areas, this is a legal obligation, even if the couple already had to consent for the marriage license. Make sure you check local laws. You can use the traditional formula of "Do you, so-and-so, take so-and-so" or you can get creative but either way, make sure you get explicit consent for the marriage during the ceremony.

There is no right way to do the vows and exchange of rings. Some couples do them at the same time, and others separately. You can use the traditional wording for the ring exchange or come up with your own. There is also no "correct" order in which a couple says their vows in a heterosexual marriage ceremony (for instance, there is no rule that the groom must go first). Don't forget to ask them to join hands. Ideally you will hold the mic for them so everyone can hear the couple.

Also, remember that vows don't have to be limited to seriousness. Inject some personality into them and they'll be much more meaningful to the couple. Vows can even be silly. I married a couple with whom I was close friends and they wanted vows that were a mix of their own jokes and a quote they loved from a television show. Get creative!

Many women these days are incorporating feminist values into their wedding ceremonies and nothing is more feminist than the marriage protest of Lucy Stone and Henry Blackwell. Lucy Stone (1818 - 1893) was a suffragist and abolitionist who kept her last name after marrying Henry Blackwell. During their wedding ceremony, both decided to register a protest in place of the vows that were traditional at the time. Though times have changed in many respects, the protest can be rewritten to reflect the ongoing struggle for equality. A straight couple I married got very creative and used this protest as a model to write their own in support of marriage equality before it became legal.

Marriage Protest of Lucy Stone and Henry Blackwell

"While we acknowledge our mutual affection by publicly assuming the relationship of husband and wife, yet in justice to ourselves and a great principle, we deem it a duty to declare that this act on our part implies no sanction of, nor promise of voluntary obedience to such of the present laws of marriage, as refuse to recognize the wife as an independent, rational being, while they confer upon the husband an injurious and unnatural superiority, investing him with legal powers which no honorable man would exercise, and which no man should possess. We protest especially against the laws which give to the husband:

1. The custody of the wife's person.
2. The exclusive control and guardianship of their children.
3. The sole ownership of her personal, and use of her real estate, unless previously settled upon her, or placed in the hands of trustees, as in the case of minors, lunatics, and idiots.
4. The absolute right to the product of her industry.
5. Also against laws which give to the widower so much larger and more permanent interest in the property of his deceased wife, than they give to the widow in that of the deceased husband.
6. Finally, against the whole system by which "the legal existence of the wife is suspended during marriage," so that in most States,

she neither has a legal part in the choice of her residence, nor can she make a will, nor sue or be sued in her own name, nor inherit property.

We believe that personal independence and equal human rights can never be forfeited, except for crime; that marriage should be an equal and permanent partnership, and so recognized by law; that until it is so recognized, married partners should provide against the radical injustice of present laws, by every means in their power."

http://www.historyisaweapon.com/defcon1/stoneblackwellmarriageprotest.html

The Ending Address to the Couple

This is now the time for you to begin shaping the bottom part of your hourglass. The couple is about to enter their new life as part of a community and this ending address is the perfect time to acknowledge this. This is usually where you write your hopes for the couple and ask their friends and family to be a support to them. You can also add a few more remarks on the meaning of relationship and its responsibilities.

The Pronouncement

And now is the moment of pronouncement! Remember that for many people, the pronouncement is the most exciting part of the wedding. The couple may have said, "Yes" and they may have said their vows and exchanged their rings but for most people, the pronouncement is the absolute signal to everyone assembled that this couple has been united in marriage.

Another Word about Our Friend, Blackstone

Some couples choose to change one or both their names and will wish to be announced as such and that is absolutely their prerogative. It is a matter of some contention about addressing a woman as "Mrs. John Doe" but do remember that if your client insists on it, it does put you in an ethical dilemma that only you can decide. Calling a woman Mrs. John Doe implies her civil death, a tradition dating back to the time in which a woman lost any civil rights she may have had upon marriage, including the right to be legally known by her own first name. To avoid this problem, I often tactfully explain to the couple the reason for my

A fitting end to any celebrant's pronouncement!

objection and offer alternatives. Remember - feminist values are humanist values!

The same problem occurs when a couple is pronounced "man and wife," the implication being that a man's station in life doesn't change regardless of marital status while a woman's position does. The alternative here is pretty clear. You can always pronounce heterosexual couples "husband and wife," "partner and partner" or another set of terms preferred by the couple. No matter who you are marrying, heterosexual or not, it is always a good idea to find out which terms the couple wants to use.

Recessional

The recessional is just what it sounds like, everyone is recessing from the front of the room to wherever they have decided to meet after the ceremony. There are more ways to do a recessional than I can even count. Some couples like a formal recessional which is the reverse order of how they processed in at the beginning, with the exception that the married couple goes first. Some couples like a more relaxed

The stressful part over, a couple lets loose on the dance floor.

atmosphere and don't want a recessional at all but rather want to stand where they are to greet guests before the party. For your part, you will want to ask beforehand how the couple wishes you to exit. I have been asked both to be part of the recessional as well as to hang back at my spot in the front of the room until everyone has exited. Whatever your couple wants to do is just right for them!

That's it! The wedding is over and everyone can now eat cake and dance!

Other Wedding Elements

Readings

Many couples like to involve family and friends in the ceremony by having them deliver readings. They may have something such as a favorite poem in mind but they may also ask you for suggestions. In some cases, they may even ask you to write or deliver the reading. If you are asked to read, just be sure that the text does not contain anything that conflicts with your personal humanist values. For instance, as the presiding celebrant and a representative of the Humanist Society, I did not, as a rule, read any religious material mentioning a deity. Though I have no personal objection to it, my role in that situation was as the representative of an organization that does not acknowledge deities. If such a reading is wanted and you feel uncomfortable, you might invite a family member or friend of the couple to deliver it instead. Again, this is a situation in which it is good to know where you stand beforehand!

It is a good idea to bring copies of the readings on the wedding day, just in case a reader forgets to bring theirs.

Music

I really love when a couple has musical friends and family! It's wonderful to include them in the ceremony, if you can. But even if everyone is tone deaf, there are still a variety of options. Just make sure you coordinate with your couple on where to place the songs within the ceremony script. Remember that music, almost more than anything else, will set the tone of the ceremony as well as serve as a bridge between other ceremony elements.

"*For couples looking for music that sounds like classical wedding music but is morecontemporary than what one may traditionally hear at a wedding, I suggest checking out the group, Vitamin String Quartet.*" [www.vitaminstringquartet.com]

— Frank Harlan, humanist celebrant, Seattle, Washington

Rituals

We may be nontheists but many of us still like our rituals! Rituals are outward symbols of important emotional or psychological experiences and many couples like to have one or more in their wedding. My own wedding involved a unity candle. Directly after our vows, my mother and my mother-in-law lit taper candles they then handed off to myself and my husband. We then lit the unity candle together which commemorated the joining of our families. I still have this beautiful brown and gold unity candle that we light on our anniversary.

Handfasting is another great ritual that comes from pagan Europe. It involves the couple wrapping or draping a cord over each other's hands

Photo will be included in May, 2018 edition

Humanist celebrant Greg Komar Storey performs a handfasting ritual.

as they recite their vows. Another way to do it is to ask the couple to join hands as you wrap them together with the ribbon. You can find traditional handfasting vows online or you can write original ones. One couple I married asked me to recite lines from Game of Thrones for their handfasting. It takes all kinds.

Wine ceremonies have exploded in popularity recently. A wine ceremony is one in which the couple pours each other a glass of wine and drinks or drinks from the same cup. There are endless variations of this ritual, including text. Check online for examples or, for a slightly boozier version, check out Frank Harlan's Aging of the Whiskey ritual at the end of this chapter.

Photo will be included in May, 2018 edition

Another ritual you may have seen at weddings recently is the sand ceremony. This is a very simple ritual meant to symbolize unity. The couple is given two different color sands and take turns pouring them into a glass jar or vase, forming a layered color effect to symbolize their coming together. Some sand ceremonies include other family members as well, each person pouring in a different color when it is their turn. At the end, all parties pour together, making a mixture of colors for the top layer. If more people are taking part than just the couple, make sure you choose a glass vessel with a large mouth! It can be difficult to have everyone pouring together at the end if there is only a small opening.

A great African American tradition is "jumping the broom." This custom originated during slavery when couples could not legally marry but instead performed folk marriages for themselves. The couple holds hands and jumps over a broom to signify the end of the ceremony and the beginning of married life.

Jewish glass breaking rituals are a great way for a Jewish couple to signify their cultural roots. This is a very simple ritual signaling the end

A newly united family celebrates their new status with a sand ceremony.

Photo will be included in May, 2018 edition

of the ceremony in which a wine glass or other thin glass is wrapped in a towel and placed before the couple as they face their guests. The couple then stomps (hard!) on the towel, safely breaking the glass without cutting themselves.

This couple chose a traditional Jewish element, that of breaking the glass.

Photographs

Some couples like to have the celebrant in the photographs, especially if you are a friend of the couple. Make sure you work out beforehand what the couple wishes from you and whether the photos will be taken before or after the ceremony. I had my own wedding photographs taken before the ceremony so that we all still looked fresh and didn't keep the party waiting! Again, the arrangements should be made according to what the couple ultimately wishes.

Real ceremony photos are also a great way to personalize your website. I suggest asking the couple if you might use one or two. If you do this, make sure you get their consent, as well as the written consent of the photographer to use them for advertising. You should do this whether the photographer is a professional or not as the photographer retains the rights to their work no matter who they are or whether the photos are "professional" or not. Don't forget to credit the photographer on your website as well. It's not just a courtesy but intellectual honesty.

The Rehearsal

The rehearsal is the last time to fine-tune your ceremony. Make sure you bring a pen with you in case you need to make any corrections to the text or any notes about timing, etc. When it comes to the rehearsal, try to make it as authentic and "real" as possible to avoid any hitches on the big day. Don't skip any readings or even music. You never know whether a reader may not know how to pronounce a word or whether the musicians know their cues. Doing it right during rehearsal means a much smoother experience on the wedding day.

Not every couple wants to have a rehearsal and some weddings are so simple that they may only need a quick couple of run-throughs before the hour. Make sure you ask your couple during consultation if they wish to have a rehearsal. Also make sure that your couples are aware if you charge extra for your presence at rehearsals. If you do, it's a good idea to have this written into your contract to avoid misunderstandings.

During the rehearsal, all participants should be made aware of their role, their cues and where they are to stand during the ceremony. In theatre, placement of the actors is called "blocking" and really, ceremony is just theatre, isn't it? As the celebrant, you are the director and your job is to make everyone feel confident about their performance. Make sure you run through the ceremony at least twice to help people remember what they need to do and where they need to be.

Be sure you arrive early to the rehearsal and locate the wedding planner, if there is one. You will want to compare notes with them to make sure you're on the same boat. Once you have done this, it is either your job to take charge and get everyone together so that you can begin. This is usually the point at which one or more overzealous family members likes to try to rearrange things because it is "traditional" to do it their way. Remember your commitment to the couple and stand firm. Don't change a thing unless the couple specifically asks you to do so.

The Wedding Day

Arrive early on the day of the wedding in case of any problems. I suggest arriving an hour before the ceremony begins. This is also the best time to get the signatures you need for the marriage license. It's nice to get these taken care of before the ceremony so that you aren't competing for attention with family and friends afterwards. Once you've obtained your signatures, make yourself scarce! People are likely flustered and running around and it's best if you stay out of the way until you're needed. Make sure to gather the wedding party fifteen minutes before the ceremony begins and have everyone in place so that the ceremony can start on time.

Signing the paperwork is sometimes incorporated into the ceremony but you can do it before or after - just make sure you get the signatures you need to make it legal!

Establish Your Boundaries Early

Wedding days are a good time for crises to arise. People are emotional, the cake hasn't arrived yet, the kids are crying … many things can go wrong! Remember that you are NOT a wedding planner and that too many cooks spoil the broth. If a crisis erupts in your domain, by all means, address it at once! But try to let the wedding planner deal with problems that are outside of your professional sphere.

Sometimes, during these crises, the couple or one of the couple may confess family secrets or problems to you. Please remember that you are NOT a counselor (and, if you by chance are a counselor, you are acting a different role this day) and refrain from giving any advice or counsel. If a client wishes you to intervene in family issues, kindly but firmly ask them to talk together and work it out.

Use Your Elevator Speech

Most often, you will be presiding over ceremonies in which many, if not most, of the guests are not humanists and, in fact, may be traditionally religious. While some may ask you to define humanism or ask related questions, refrain from disparaging anyone's religion or debating religion with anyone. Remember to conduct yourself professionally and put yourself in charge of giving everyone present a warm, positive experience of humanism!

Don't Forget Your Survival Kit!

On the day of the wedding, you will want to equip yourself with the following items:

- At least two copies of the ceremony (just in case!)
- A portfolio or other professional-looking cover from which to read the ceremony
- A pen for any last-minute changes
- A bottle of water – you'll be doing a lot of speaking!

- Tissues
- Touch up makeup if you wear it
- A hairbrush/comb
- Your certificate or state-issued papers showing that you are a legal officiant
- Your certificate issued by the Humanist Society showing that you have been endorsed
- Your business cards
- A stamped, addressed envelope for the license (you can mail it on your way out)

Wedding Ceremony Excerpt Examples

Sometimes you just need a little inspiration to get started. Check out these real-life wedding ceremony excerpts and examples submitted by ministers and celebrants from all over North America. They include everything from short and sweet ceremonies to longer, more formal ceremonies with interesting elements. Please use these examples only for inspiration as they represent the original work of their authors.

The scripts are written so that they are easy to understand. For instance, all "blocking" or physical movement by the wedding party is in brackets whereas comments are in parentheses, just like a play script. The speaker of each part is in bold. When the author of the ceremony has added a prologue, it is in italics at the beginning of the script and provides helpful background information.

Full Ceremony Examples

A Quick but Formal Wedding Ceremony

Sometimes couples want to have something special to mark the day but don't want to sit through a long ceremony. In that case, a quick but meaningful wedding service may be appropriate. But even a quick ceremony has room for personalization. The two ceremonies that follow are quite different from each other. The first, written by my friend Kathy for her own wedding, is cute, fun, and very much in keeping with the culture of the city of Richmond, Virginia. Kenna Covington follows up with a ceremony that is simple but elegant. So, remember that even if your ceremony will be short on words, there is still plenty of room to make it special!

Kathy Greenier, Richmond, Virginia

Opening Words

Celebrant: "Family and friends, welcome! Today, we gather in charming, creative Richmond, Virginia to bear witness to the marriage of Kathy and Alex. Thank you for being here to celebrate the love that Kathy and Alex share--a love that is joyful, trusting, and purposefully effortful. As a friend of the couple, I'm especially honored to serve as the officiant for this ceremony."

"I met Kathy and Alex through mutual friends and was delighted to learn that we lived in the same neighborhood of Church Hill. Over the last year, we've become closer through monthly book club meetings, backyard fire pits, and one rainy camping trip. Throughout knowing them, I've been touched by the very special affection they share, as well as the deeply caring, ongoing commitment they make to one another through their words and actions."

Readings

Celebrant: "Now, Alex's Dad T will read a poem he wrote to commemorate this occasion, and Kathy's friends M, M, and K will share readings by feminist theorist bell hooks, from her treatise "All About Love: New Visions"."

(Participants give readings)

Vows

Celebrant: "Surrounded by all of you, family and friends, Alex and Kathy will now make shared vows."

"Alex and Kathy, do you swear to be supportive, compassionate, generous, and patient with each other as you grow together?"

Couple: "We do."

Celebrant: "Do you pledge to empower each other and celebrate each other's differences? Do you promise to respect each other's independence - to continue to build your relationship as individuals, partners, and as equals?"

Couple: "We do."

Celebrant: "Do you promise to communicate openly and honestly and to always try to help the other understand you?"

Couple: "We do."

Celebrant: "Do you commit to seeking happiness, laughter, and adventure - together - exploring the things you have yet to learn and places you have yet to go?"

Couple: "We do."

Celebrant: "Please exchange rings and hold hands. Repeat after me to express your intent, "I, Kathy/Alex, choose you as my husband/wife. I ask you to be none other than yourself. I love you for who you are, for who you might become, and for who I am when I am with you."

The Pronouncement

Celebrant: "I am delighted to pronounce you husband and wife! Kiss!"

Kenna Covington of North Carolina Secular Weddings

A Simple Wedding Ceremony - Opening Words

Celebrant: "Thank you all for joining us today on this beautiful day. You have traveled to be with the people you love, to share with RR and MC as they publicly declare their love and commitment with one another in marriage."

"Welcome, R and M. We are all glad to be with you today as you take this step in your lifelong love story. You know what it takes to make a relationship thrive; you've done it for a while now. Your love for one another has brought you closer than you've ever been with another."

"Every day you leave your home wearing the other's love, like a beacon of light and a suit of armor for and in the world. You know that love isn't a state of perfect caring, it is an active noun, like struggle; to love someone is to strive to accept that person exactly the way he or she is, right here, and now."

"You are here today to share the depth of your love, friendship, appreciation, and respect for each other, and your desire to be together for the rest of your days. After today, you will tell the world that this is the person I am most comfortable with – the one who gets me; this is my husband, this is my wife."

Vows

Celebrant: "R and M, you have carefully considered the beauty of the obligations assumed when lives are wed. Are you prepared to enter into this covenant of marriage?"

Couple: "We are."

Celebrant: "R, do you to take M as your husband for the rest of your days?"

Bride: "I do."

Celebrant: "M, do you take R as your wife for the rest of your days?"

Groom: "I do."

Celebrant: "Wedding vows are promises, ideas, and values that shape our lives. When you are ready, please repeat after me. R, you can go first."

"M, I take you as you are

Loving who you are now

And who you are yet to become.

I promise to listen to you

And learn from you.

To support you

And accept your support.

I will celebrate your triumphs

And mourn your losses

As though they were my own.

I will love you

And have faith in your love for me

Through all our years

And all that life may bring us."

(Bride repeats vows).

Celebrant: "Good job. Now, M, it's your turn."

"R, I take you as you are

Loving who you are now

And who you are yet to become.

I promise to listen to you

And learn from you.

To support you

And accept your support.

I will celebrate your triumphs

And mourn your losses

As though they were my own.

I will love you

And have faith in your love for me

Through all our years

And all that life may bring us."

(Groom repeats vows)

Exchange of Rings

Celebrant: "May we please have the rings?"

"Above you the stars, below you the stones, before you, the passing of time. Like a star, let your love be constant. Like a stone, let your love be durable. Like the passing of time, let your love be generous and unafraid."

"The metal in these rings is precious. Unearthed, heated, shaped, and polished – to create them an artisan made something where there was nothing before."

"Love is like that. It comes from humble beginnings, and through a combination of serendipity and effort, imperfect beings shape it into something extraordinary. It's the process of making something beautiful where there was once nothing at all."

"These rings are an ideal symbol of your love for each other and a physical reminder that the permanence of your union is in your hands."

"M, will you please place the ring you present to R on her left hand and let her know that you are honored to marry her."

[Groom places ring on bride's finger]

Celebrant: "R, will you please place the ring you present to M on his left hand and let him know that you are honored to marry him."

[Bride places ring on groom's finger]

Celebrant: "M and R, your hearts and minds are bound to each other, your intentions and words are entwined, your rings have been given and accepted. By the power vested in me, I pronounce you married, as husband and wife. Please share your first kiss as a married couple."

A Destination Wedding

What is more romantic than a beach wedding? Victoria Gipson was honored to be asked to officiate the wedding of two friends on a gorgeous beach in Texas. She used the occasion to weave some ocean imagery into her poetic words.

Victoria Gipson of Secular Celebrations of Northeast Indiana

Opening Words

Celebrant: "As the tides ebb and flow so do the fortunes of life.
Footprints in the sand are washed away.
Driftwood moves on to its endless quest for a peaceful harbor.
Only a deep and abiding love can withstand the tides of change in the lives of two people."

Intent to Marry

Celebrant: "Is it your intent today to join together as friends, as lovers, as husband and wife? If so say, "Yes, it is!"
(Couple responds)

Vows

(Couple is asked to take a hold of each other's hands)

Celebrant: "Do you pledge to reach for these hands and look to these eyes to comfort you and be your safe harbor when the seas of life toss you about? If so say, "we do!"

(Couple responds)

Celebrant: "When you are blessed with fair winds, when sunshine kisses your face, when good fortune smiles upon your individual and joint endeavors will you pledge to run to each other's arms in celebration? If so say, "we do!"

(The couple now share heartfelt words written for each other)

Exchange of Rings

(The couple takes turns reciting while exchanging rings)
I give you this ring,
as a symbol of my love,
my confidence in our strength together,
and my covenant,
to learn and grow with you.

Officiant's Well Wishes for the Couple

Celebrant: "My Wish for you both is that your love and commitment to one another will remain as powerful and endless as this sea that is before us today and that your occasions for laughter and joy will be as numerous as the grains of sand that are now beneath your feet."

Declaration of Marriage

Celebrant: "By virtue of the love you have for one another and by virtue of the authority vested in me under the laws of the State of Texas it gives me great honor and pleasure to pronounce you husband and wife!"

A Wedding with Audience Participation

Kenna Covington of North Carolina Secular Weddings (who does other non-wedding ceremonies too!) always has something interesting to add. The script that follows involves a little help from the audience to warm up the rings!

Kenna Covington of North Carolina Secular Weddings

Opening Words

Celebrant: "Good evening; thank you for joining us. Our bride and groom have asked that you please silence your mobile devices and keep your cameras and phones in your pockets in order to be fully present during the ceremony. Thank you; a beautiful ceremony is about to begin."

[Procession enters and celebrant asks guests to be seated]

Celebrant: "Welcome, family and friends! It is wonderful to be with you this evening at the 1870 Farm in Chapel Hill, North Carolina. We have gathered to witness and celebrate with EW and BA. As couples have done for thousands of years, these two come before you to make a promise that binds them across all previous boundaries; they come before you to join their lives in marriage."

"We aren't here today to mark the start of a relationship; however, we are here to recognize a bond that already exists – that began with a boy who fell in love with a beautiful girl and her amazing smile, countless acts of kindness, an amazing amount of patience, and an abundance of learning. Deep consideration, the desire to be connected, and immeasurable amounts of laughter, learning, and love have brought E and B to this moment.

A ceremony like this weaves us into the larger, tapestry of our families and friends. Each one of you has also played an integral part in bringing B and E to this moment. This transition is important to them and they are honored to be surrounded by you - the most important people in their lives. And tonight, when your feet hurt from all the dancing, and your cheeks ache from so much laughter, you will return to your homes – and in your own ways, will continue to support and contribute to their relationship."

Ring Warming

[Two attendants hold up the rings while celebrant is speaking, hold them for a moment and then pass them to the attendant beside them. Once the final attendants have held the rings for a moment, they will take them to the guests in the back and give them instructions on how to pass the rings (crisscross and then to the row ahead of them).

Celebrant: "One of the ways we'll be celebrating the closeness of those gathered here is with a ring warming. This is something you may not have seen before, but it's a wonderfully romantic sentiment that will help give B and E's rings even more meaning today. We'll send the rings through the bridal party - attendants will bring them to you at the back. Please take a moment to hold the ring and fill them with your love, your well wishes, your prayers, and blessings, before passing it to the person next to you. If we do this right, the rings will meet a few times before they are passed to our mothers of the bride and groom, who will bring them forward when the time is right."

"E and B, we are all so glad to be with you on the beautiful day. On this day, the world is celebrating the earth, and here we are, beneath a tree – older than anyone can remember, sharing this moment with you as you join your lives together. Take a moment. Breathe it all in – every bit of sacrificing and planning, decision making and bringing it all together – it's been worth it. You can it feel from everyone around you – loving you both and cheering you on."

"For a while now, you've been growing your own roots - with each other, your families, friends, and your wider community. You've built a strong foundation for your relationship based on honesty and respect. You have found joy in each other's company, and you have become better, more fulfilled people because of your connection. You've experienced more life through the other's eyes and found a deeper meaning to your own. This experience has taught you that love isn't always like fireworks; that those who truly love, have roots that grow towards each other underground - in the spaces no one else will ever see. And, when all the pretty blossoms have fallen from their branches, they find that they are one tree and not two.

That's why we are here today; everyone gathered here is a witness to you as you publicly tell the world that you choose to stand together as equal partners - that your roots have grown together. Each complementing the other - you've found that your love, and the life you've created from love, is something neither of you wants to live without. Your beautiful friendship, has been earned, offered, and shared."

"In eleven years, you've laughed more than you can recall. You've supported one another and watched each other strive for and accomplish their goals. You've struggled and overcome more adversity than you thought you ever could, and you've learned more than your younger selves could have ever imagined. Eleven years is a drop in the bucket of your very long and loving marriage that begins today."

[Celebrant turns toward groom]. "After today, you'll tell the world that this is the most beautiful woman in the world and she personifies tenacity, compassion, wisdom, and kindness – she sees the best in me even when I can't see it in myself; she trusts with her whole heart and shows me every day just how good people can be – this is my wife. "

[Celebrant turns toward bride]. "And after today, you'll tell the world that this is the hard-working man who makes me feel safe and secure, who is kind and thoughtful, who will always go the extra mile for me and our family, who challenges and inspires me – this is my husband."

"The world is so full of love and moral depth, and we remain grateful every day for the brief but magnificent opportunity that life provides. The sum of all our efforts, our thinking, and our accomplishments is love."

"There is no doubt that you have carefully considered the beauty of the obligations assumed when lives are wed. B and E, are you ready to exchange vows and become husband and wife?"

Couple: "We are."

Vows and Exchange of Rings

Celebrant: "Wedding Vows are promises, values, and ideas that shape our shared lives. Today, your friends and family are here, vowing their support and connection."

"Have our rings made their way through our group?" (When rings reach the mothers of the couple, continue with the script below)

"We have come to the point in our ceremony where B and E will exchange these rings. They were created by a loved one, and have been imbued with your blessings and love. Mothers, will you please bring the rings to B and E?"

[Mothers give the rings to E and B who hold their rings for reflection.]

Celebrant: "Traditionally, the passage to the status of husband and wife is marked by the exchange of rings. These rings connect you to one another, to all who are gathered here, to the planet, and to the universe. The elements in these rings is precious to us. Your rings are an excellent representation of the sentiment you are sharing today, that like the elements in these rings, love comes from humble beginnings - and through a combination of serendipity and effort, imperfect beings shape it into something extraordinary."

"Wearing these rings will remind you of the commitment you have made to one another, the love that surrounds you both, and that the permanence of your union is in your own hands."

"B, as you place the ring on E's finger, please repeat after me:
E, I give you this ring
As a symbol of our love.
It carries my best intentions.
I am honored to be your husband."

"E, as you place the ring on B's finger, please repeat after me:

B, I give you this ring

As a symbol of our love.

It carries my best intentions.

I am honored to be your wife."

Pronouncement

Celebrant: "The purpose of our gathering is fulfilled. We have witnessed the promises of love, mutual respect, and commitment given by E and B to live together as husband and wife for all of their days."

"May you find life richer for journeying through it together."

"By the power vested in me by the Humanist Society and the state of North Carolina, it is my great honor to pronounce you are married as husband and wife."

"And now, you may kiss!"

"Friends and family, please join me in great cheer as I introduce to you for the first time, B and E 2.0!

[Wedding party exits]

Instructions to Guests

Celebrant: "Thank you for joining us for the ceremony. E and B are married and all is well in the world. It's a beautiful evening and our bridal party will join us in a few moments after they take some photos. In the meantime, please join us in the barn and enjoy cocktail hour. Thank you so much."

Ceremony or Ritual Excerpts

In the following script, D. G. gives us a great example of a ceremony with an emphasis on equality of both bride and groom in a heterosexual union.

D. G. Van Curen, humanist celebrant, Boise, Idaho

D. G. says, "In times long past, marriage was not an equal partnership and such was reflected in the language of the wedding ceremony. Many such subtle references, like the opening statement "Who gives this woman to this man in marriage", are still found in traditional weddings. For many in this modern era, the master/subservient language is unacceptable. The following is an example of a modern equality cere-mony, giving bride and groom equal status throughout."

Processional:

(Two entry points are needed for this. If the venue has two back doors (corners), then two aisles are made, starting at the back corners (entries) and proceeding at an angle to the altar, creating a "V" shape, back to front. Seating can be easily arranged to create this formation. Bridesmaids, unescorted, walk down one aisle, while groomsmen down the other. Timing enhances the appearance, so the pace down both aisles should be such that pairs (one bridesmaid and one groomsmen, for example) arrive at the front at the same time, and take their places. Lastly, the groom and bride enter at the same time, walking down the different aisles and arriving at the front at the same time. As an alter-native processional, the two groups can begin at opposing side entries, walking in front of the seated guests.)

(Music stops and officiant then begins).

Opening Words

Celebrant: "Are you both, this day and before all present, ready to accept each other in marriage?"

Couple: "We are."

Celebrant: "Dear friends and family, we are gathered here today to witness and celebrate the union of _____ and _____ in marriage. Over time, they have come to realize that their personal dreams, hopes, and goals are more attainable and more meaningful through the combined effort and mutual support provided in love and commitment, and so they have now decided to live together as husband and wife."

Celebrant: "The little things are the big things. It is never being too old to hold hands. It is remembering to say "I love you" at least once a day. It is never going to sleep angry. It is at no time taking the other for granted; the courtship should not end with the honeymoon, it should continue through all the years. It is having a mutual sense of values and common objectives; it is facing the world together. It is forming a circle of love that gathers in the whole family. It is doing things for each other, not in the attitude of duty or sacrifice, but the spirit of joy. It is speaking words of appreciation and demonstrating gratitude in thoughtful ways. It is not expecting the husband to wear a halo or the wife to have the wings of an angel. It is not looking for perfection in each other. It is cultivating flexibility, patience, understanding, and a sense of humor. It is having the capacity to forgive and forget. It is giving each other an atmosphere in which each can grow. It is finding room for the things of the spirit. It is the common search for the good and the beautiful. It is the establishing of a relationship in which the independence is equal, the dependence is mutual, and the obligation is reciprocal."

Vows

Celebrant: "In the presence of our family and friends, I vow to be your conscientious partner in sickness and in health, in good times and in bad, and in joy as well as in sorrow. I promise to love you unconditionally, to support you in your goals and pursuits, to honor and respect you, to laugh with you and cry with you, and to cherish you for as long as we both shall live."

"Do you, _____, accept _____ as your partner in life, in sickness and in health, in good times and bad, in joy as well as sorrow, to love (her/him) unconditionally, to support (her/him) in (her/his) goals and pursuits, to honor and respect (her/him), to laugh with (her/him) and cry with (her/him), and to cherish (her/him for as long as you both shall live?"

Couple: "I do."Frank Harlan of Seattle, Washington really enjoys the ceremony as production. He has an eye for stage blocking and props so no wonder he provided us with three great examples of rituals celebrants can use to give their ceremonies a special quality! What follows is a unity ritual, a touching family blending ritual, and a wonderful little family ritual called "Three Promises."

Frank Harlan, humanist celebrant, Seattle, Washington

Unity Ritual: Ageing of the Whiskey

"For me, as a Celebrant and wedding ceremony producer, a wedding ceremony is a performance, and I see a concept like a Unity Ritual to be a transformative piece in the performance. I place it following Vows and

Ring Exchange and right before the closing message and pronounce-ment. I like to set and display the Unity Ritual props to the right or left side of the staging area and invite the couple to join me there when it comes time to present it. For this ritual, you'll need a whiskey making kit and a high-top table."

Celebrant: Now, that you have declared your affirmations of love and exchanged rings, it is time to perform a task together ... please join me.

[Couple and Celebrant move the table holding the props and take their position on opposite sides of the table, facing guests.]

Celebrant: Today, Partners A and B have chosen to commemorate their marriage with a contemporary Unity Ritual, the "Ageing of the Whiskey." The magic that happens inside of a whiskey barrel is symbol-ic of what happens between two people who are committed to an inti-mate lifetime of love with each other. This transformation of un-aged whiskey through the various stages of its evolution has always intrigued whiskey drinkers. The transformation from undrinkable to full maturity is accomplished by putting the life-force of the distillate into the tiny oak barrel; a micro-illustration of a lifetime shared.

[Celebrant acknowledges and points out the tiny oak barrel]

Celebrant: "The bond between the un-aged whiskey and the wooden barrel is similar to the bond created by two people who are truly committed to their partnership. It's next to impossible to witness the depth of the transformations that take place in a couple's hearts -- as with the distillate, the transformation from clear to brown."

"For this ritual, the two individual bottles of un-aged whiskey -- also known as "white dog," or "white lightning," by some distillers and "moonshine" by others -- sitting on the table represent your separate lives, your separate families, and your separate sets of friends."

"Each bottle is strong, independent and can potentially become a perfect bottle of aged whiskey on its own. However, when the two bottles are merged together with intention, they represent an entirely new and unique relationship."

"Partners A and B, please pick up the bottle of "white dog" next to you."

[Each person picks up and hold their bottles of white dog whiskey.]

Celebrant: "Partner B, the bottle of white dog whiskey you hold represents your life before today. It symbolizes all that you are and all that you can ever be as an individual. Please pour yourself into the empty wooden barrel on the table."

[Partner B pours the bottle of un-aged whiskey into the wooden barrel and sets the empty bottle on the table]

Celebrant: "Partner A, the bottle of white dog whiskey you hold also represents your life before today. It symbolizes all that you are and all that you can ever be as an individual. Add yourself into the wooden barrel on the table."

[Partner A pours the bottle of un-aged whiskey into the wooden barrel and sets the empty bottle on the table]

Celebrant: "Will the two of you please complete the process and seal the barrel."

[Partner B tops the barrel off with filtered water (roughly 12 oz.). This will bring the whiskey down to 84-85 proof which is optimal drinking strength]

[Partner A inserts the bung ensuring an airtight seal and writes the date on the face of the barrel]

[Partners A and B stay standing together behind table]

Celebrant: "As the whiskey ages over the next few months, the extracts from the wood will make the taste of the whiskey become more complex – let the process of Ageing the Whiskey be a reminder of the vows you have made to one another today. Like any good relationship, I hope that the merging of your spirits continues to bring out the many flavors, aromas, and complexities in taste that will take place during your lifetime journey together." In the next three to four months, your whiskey will be evolving into something very special."

"How will you know it is ready to enjoy? The same way you will make any other important life decision from this day on, together."

"Let the Ageing of the Whiskey remind you that everything can always be good because the two of you are in control of your destiny. Like this one-of- a kind-barrel of whiskey, I hope that your time together on this earth, allows your relationship to be aged to perfection."

[Celebrant invites couple to return to their places and ceremony continues.]

Unity Ritual: Family Blending

"Whenever a child or children are a part of a couple's union I always suggest they include a Family Blending Ritual. Below is the outline I use for scripting a Family Blending Ritual. I usually place it after the Exchange of Rings. This script is from a wedding ceremony where the groom was a single dad with a son."

Celebrant: "Let it be known that Partners A and B do not enter this union alone. Partner A brings with him an amazing and vibrant 13-year old son. (Child's First Name), will you please come forward and stand between your Father and Partner B."

"Over the years, you have gotten to know each other; sharing meals, hanging out, and just spending time together. You have successfully melded into a modern-day family. Today (Child's First Name), your support to this marriage is clear. Partner B joins this family circle as your father's wife, as a friend that you can count on, and as a woman who loves both of you very much."

"I would like to tell all of you some things that Partners A and B think all of you should know about this amazing young person (Child's Full Birth Name)."

"Your Father tells me…"

(Parent to provide a list of 2-3 qualities they recognize and admire about their child)

"And Partner B shared with me that…"

(Partner B to provide a list of 2-3 qualities they recognize and admire about the child)

Optional: Commemorative Gift

"As a way to commemorate this momentous occasion, your Father and Partner B have a gift for you, and they would like to present it to you now, is that okay?"

(Parents give gift to child)

The Goodrich family incorporated a family blending ritual of the sand ceremony to signify two families coming together as one.

Family Blessing

("I always close the ritual with a message for the family and a group hug before asking the child/children to return to their seats.")

Celebrant: "Please take hands."

"(Father, Partner B and Child's Name), I ask that your home be a place of happiness for all who enter it, and a place where the old and the young are renewed in each other's company, a place for growing, a place for music and celebration, a place for laughter and goofing off. And when life seems to be too much or you just had a rough day, may your home always be a place of refuge where every one of you can find the comfort of always knowing that you will be accepted and loved unconditionally."

Option Element: Three Promises from the Children

(When both partners have children, these are promises the kids make to the family unit. The couple usually very happy to come up with the three questions so that they relate to their children and their family. For the staging, the kids are standing in front of or between their parents).

Celebrant: "(List Child(ren) by first Name(s) I am going to ask you three questions. I would like all of you to answer each of them with, "I Promise!"

"Do you promise to be tolerant, respectful and accepting of each other's differences?"

Kids: "I Promise!"

Celebrant: "Do you promise to always work out disagreements so that your friendships can grow stronger?"

Kids: "I Promise!"

Celebrant: "Do you promise to keep your rooms clean and the dirty dishes out of the basement?"

Kids: "I Promise!"

Option Element: Three Promises for the Adults and Child(ren)

Celebrant: "Mother/Father, Partner and Child(ren) would you please join hands. I am going to ask all of you three questions. I would like all of you to answer each of them with, 'I Promise!'"

"Do you promise to love, respect and protect each other from this day forward?"

Family: "I Promise!"

Celebrant: "Do you promise to always try to be the best person you can be?

Family: "I Promise!"

Celebrant: Do you promise to accept the responsibility of being a family, and encourage, and support each other in your new life together?

Family: "I Promise!"

Unitarian Universalist minister Anne Barker is what I like to think of as an expert in empathy. She has a way of simply and yet profoundly capturing the meaning of moments. Here is an excerpt of some opening words for a wedding ceremony.

Anne Barker, Unitarian Universalist Minister, Edmonton, Alberta

"Sacred: I use this word to mean 'highly valued, full of meaning', rather than 'affirmed by some supernatural code'. 'Tender' also works. I like sacred. Ask your people."

Celebrant:

There is no time more open

Where we choose to be fully present

Than the moments of ritual

To one another

and to a sacred promise.

This is a new beginning...

A transition between what was and what will be.

Your union, (name and name),

Is also an invitation for each one of us

To reflect upon our own choices ...

To renew our vows to our beloved ...

To honor our own transitions,

With a moment of pause and reflection ...

Within this gentle calm that you have created.

To restore our spirits,

This open space of ritual

Is not only for these two people.

It is also for each person present

That each of us will choose

How we might pass through.

Creating a doorway

For this gift, we thank you.

Patrick McGraw shows us that science is not dull and emotionless but instead inspiration for our most memorable moments! This excerpt is a great example of how humanists can translate their deep awe for nature into an expression of love.

Patrick McGraw, humanist celebrant, St. Louis, Missouri

(Quotes are from Carl Sagan's *A Pale Blue Dot*)

Celebrant: "Ashley, Brittany, you fell in love by chance. Countless factors had to align correctly for you two to find one another. But you are here today because you are making a choice, perhaps the greatest choice that any of us can make; the choice to share your lives."

"I would like to share a little story."

"On February 14th, (Valentine's Day!) 1990, a descendant of humanity, Voyager 1 had completed its primary mission and was on its way out of our star system. At a distance of about 6 billion kilometers, (or 3.7 billion miles), Carl Sagan convinced NASA to command the little robot to turn its camera back and take one last photograph. In that now famous photo, our planet can be seen as but a single pixel - a Pale Blue Dot."

"Of that photograph, Carl would later write:

"Look again at that dot. That's here. That's home. That's us. On it everyone you love, everyone you know, everyone you ever heard of, every human being who ever was, lived out their lives. The aggregate of our joy and suffering, thousands of confident religions, ideologies, and economic doctrines, every hunter and forager, every hero and coward, every creator and destroyer of civilization, every king and peasant, every young couple in love, every mother and father, hopeful child, inventor and explorer, every teacher of morals, every corrupt politician, every "superstar," every "supreme leader," every saint and sinner in the history of our species lived there -- on a mote of dust suspended in a sunbeam."

"Our posturing, our imagined self-importance, the delusion that we have some privileged position in the universe, are challenged by this point of pale light. Our planet is a lonely speck in the great enveloping cosmic dark. In our obscurity, in all this vastness, there is no hint that help will come from elsewhere to save us from ourselves."

"I have always found the insignificance of us to be incredibly inspiring. We are flecks of carbon clinging to the crust of a tiny pebble spinning in the vastness of space. Our existence is only the tiniest blink in all of the universe. One life. One chance. It is for that very reason that how we choose to use the precious, fleeting moment of our lives is all the more important. Those who manage to make or find a purpose in their time create their own reward. Those who find someone with whom to share this treasure are truly fortunate."

"You two are choosing to share your moment - dedicating yourselves to making one another's lives better, happier, and healthier."

> I hope that these examples show you just how varied, expressive, and interesting humanist wedding ceremonies can be. There is so much material to work with, both in the world around us and within our philosophical tradition. Humanists don't have to settle for a courthouse wedding anymore!

CHAPTER 4

Humanist Funeral and Memorial Services

There has been a huge upswing in demand for funerals and memorials that more accurately reflect the life of loved ones than is usually found in more traditionally religious ceremonies. Religious funerals, while not totally ignoring the unique life of the person, often focus primarily on the afterlife and on distinctly theistic rituals. A humanist funeral or memorial service, however, is entirely about the person whose life is being celebrated. Though more and more people are choosing a nonreligious end-of-life ceremony, many more still don't realize that this option is open to them and expect to have their ceremonies in a church or in a funeral home with a rote service that will likely have religious or theistic overtones. S. B. Collins, a humanist celebrant in Washington who uses they/them pronouns, knows this problem personally.

When S. B.'s grandfather died, he was given a funeral home service. S. B.'s uncle turned to them and said, "He'd be so pissed to know that we're here!" From that point on, S. B. made it their mission to educate people about the more personalized options available to them. "I want to change the way we look at death in American society," they said. For S. B., that includes providing the client's family with the choice of a home funeral, among other things. Just as with a humanist wedding ceremony, we can let the needs of the clients and the clients' family dictate the style and setting of a funeral or memorial service without worrying about religious customs or rules.

A word about definitions: a funeral is usually more accurately described as an interment. That is, the body of the deceased is present and will be interred during or immediately after the ceremony. A memorial takes place without the body of the deceased present, often after they have been cremated or buried.

And yet, while more people are looking for secular or nontheistic alternatives to traditional funerals and memorials, finding the expertise can be difficult. Though funerals and memorials are not legal ceremonies and therefore, anyone can perform them, many people will prefer to have a professional take the helm. But many humanist celebrants and officiants decline to do funerals because they are emotionally taxing and because, unlike a wedding, minor slip-ups aren't very funny. This can make the thought of performing a funeral or memorial nerve-wracking to a celebrant.

However, those celebrants who do take on the task often report that offering these services can be extremely rewarding and meaningful for them personally. Ian Bushfield, executive director of the BC Humanists, says that he gets satisfaction knowing that even for just a few hours, he can take the burden of management from a grieving family's shoulders.

You might wonder, how could I ever do a memorial service? What would I say when I only have a day or so at most to capture the entire life of an individual? What if I cry? What if I mess up my words? What if

I'm asked to do the funeral of a child? Or for someone who has committed suicide?

These are all very normal questions and fears but don't let it stop you from offering this vital service to your community. I say vital because a good funeral or memorial service should remind the living of what's truly worth living for – relationship, truth, beauty, meaning. I think that funerals and memorials should really be the most important element of humanist celebrancy. As a philosophy, humanism is focused on discovering during this lifetime what really matters to us and how we can use our lives to enrich others. A positive cultural relationship with death and grief can help spur us on to thinking about what truly matters. In celebrating the life of someone who has died, we are all reminded of what we really live for and it is not money, accomplishments, or status. As Alain de Botton says, "Contemplating our mortality may give us the courage to unhook our lives from the more gratuitous of society's expectations."[9] And so, you see, funerals and memorials are indeed for the living. Good humanism, like good religion, should help us to realize through our grief what it is we're living for.

Many people are looking for humanistic funerals but don't quite know where to find a celebrant or even that having such a memorial is an option. I encourage you to put yourself out there and let people know that you can help them navigate this difficult time without the baggage of unwanted theism.

Performing a humanist funeral or memorial service is much the same in function as officiating a humanist wedding service. You, as the celebrant, are facilitating a positive and emotional ritual centered on the lives of your clients or the clients' loved one. You will use the same skills: writing, speaking, dealing with family members and guests, and you will need to follow proper business procedures as you would with any wedding contract.

Types of Clients

There are two different kinds of clients you will meet as a humanist celebrant who performs funerals and memorials. There is the client who is arranging their own service to prepare for the future, and there is the client who is arranging for an immediate service for someone who has just died. The client whose funeral or memorial is imminent is often referred to as an "in need" or "at need" client. Those planning ahead are called "pre-need" clients.

Celebrant Kathy Deidrich performed the memorial service of Maria (Reit) Boers, an immigrant from The Netherlands. The lovely tulip wreath, made by her granddaughter, was placed around her urn in honor of her heritage.

Consultation

"Perhaps the toughest part about performing a humanist memorial is learning so much about someone who you'll never get to meet. Speaking with the survivors, the ones who cared for and loved the deceased so dearly, and doing so while they're still in the grieving process is heart-wrenching. But I think there's a certain importance to it. Being able to talk through the story of someone you've lost provides some closure and the ceremony itself represents a nice symbolic closure. As a Humanist Officiant, I'm able to take the responsibility for that event off those who are grieving and allow them to process their emotions. It's a tough but ultimately rewarding experience."

- Ian Bushfield, Humanist Officiant and Executive Director of the British Columbia Humanist Association

For the more immediate funeral or memorial service, you will, of course, want to meet with your client, often a family member, as soon as possible. Most funerals take place within three days of death and while a memorial service can take place at any time, it is best for the grieving process that it happens sooner rather than later. Arrange to meet with your client as soon as it is convenient for you both. The consultation is a great opportunity to meet the family and also to gather information about the person whose life you will be celebrating. It's likely that you will not be speaking as much as listening during a funeral or memorial consultation and your client may be emotionally distressed. Remember to be patient and only interject when you need clarification. As always, remember that you are not a counselor. Allowing someone to talk can be therapeutic but you should refrain from putting yourself into the role of an actual therapist. In other words, stay in your lane. You can always refer your client to a therapist if the need arises.

As the client speaks, take notes. They will be eager to tell you all about their loved one, all of the achievements, funny memories, and sad stories. It will give them comfort to talk about their friend or family member and you will be getting to know the life you're celebrating. Be sure to find out personal information such as nicknames or other personal details which will help to make the service unique to them. Ask whether family or friends would like an active role in the service. Perhaps they might want to read a poem or tell a story. If the latter, make sure you coordinate with the speakers so that you are not all telling the same stories over and over again. Most importantly, make sure you are certain of when and where the funeral is to take place and, if it will be in a funeral home, be sure to stop by and introduce yourself to the director and get a sense of the space you'll be using.

A further important detail is whether the deceased was a humanist or simply nonreligious. If they were a humanist, you might want to include specifically humanist content such as an explanation of their belief system as something that was important to them or their involvement in humanist groups or causes. Or, you as the celebrant may want to highlight humanist philosophy as it relates to living and dying. A nonreligious service is not the same as an explicitly humanist one.

The pre-planning client is a slightly different situation in that you will be speaking directly to the person whose funeral or memorial you'll be doing. Though the resulting ceremony will be similar to the at-need client, the timeline is usually longer and there is benefit to speaking directly with the person whose service you will be performing. When speaking to someone who is pre-planning or to their representative, you may find that they already have ideas about what they want. However, you will just as likely encounter someone who knows only that they do not want a traditionally religious ceremony. Your job is to help them navigate this most difficult time and provide a space for their wishes to be known and executed. When you are with a client who is unsure how to proceed, calmly take the reins by making some suggestions. Ask about songs, artwork, poetry, etc. that is important and significant to them. Ask them about the moments that meant the most in their lives and about people they love. Ask about significant milestones in their lives and places they've lived or traveled. You'll soon find that you have plenty of material to work with.

Pro Tip

Talking with a dying person about their own funeral can be extremely difficult. Just remember that a pre-need client contacts you because he or she wants to take part in this process and they are usually glad you're there to help ease the burden on the family they leave behind.

To give you a little help, UU minister Anne Barker has some useful suggestions when consulting with clients.

Anne Barker, Unitarian Universalist Minister, Edmonton, Alberta

Sample Celebration of Life / Memorial / Funeral Questions:

If I am doing the eulogy, the interview is more complicated and requires the second set of questions provided below under "Additional Eulogy Details." If someone else (or a few people) are telling the person's life story, then the first set of questions is usually enough. I ask for a copy of the obituary and links to other public documents like the person's blog, website, tributes, etc. If other people are participating in the service, I require that their readings, eulogies, songs, etc. are sent to me in advance, and I include their words in my service booklet. This allows me to have a complete record of the service for the family, to ensure that the others are prepared ahead of time, and that I have a copy in case they break down and want me to read their words for them. Most importantly, people often change their plan, adding or excluding items that I was expecting to cover or leave out. Having their notes ahead of time allows me to edit my work, providing a cohesive whole.

Consultation Questions

Tell me about your loved one. (The most important thing is to encourage people to share their stories – small stories of poignant events, throughout the service, make it unique and special.)

What is each of your relationship to _____?

Do you have words that you would like to say about _____? (or that you would like me to read?)

Where were they born (family details: parents, siblings, school, work, etc.)

Tell me about their education, work and/or home life. (don't assume they worked)

What were their interests? How did they spend their time? (hobbies, passions, volunteer work, etc.)

What about... (or Can you say more about...) their significant relationships? (spouses, children, business partners, close friends....)

What kind of a _____ were they? (parent, partner, friend, worker, athlete, etc.)

How do you think they would want to be remembered?

What is the tone or mood you would like for this remembrance?

Are there special songs or readings that you would like to include – maybe something that was a favorite of your loved one, or that reflects how you feel about them?

Do you want an open microphone during the ceremony?

What else would you like me to know about _____?

What are your plans for a final resting place? (Cremation / burial / urn at home / etc.) Do you want this information shared with the guests?

(Guests often ask "will there be a graveside service?" or "where will ____'s ashes be spread? If it's not in the obituary, it can save the family a lot of questions if plans are shared in the service. However, some people want to keep this information private – so I never share it without asking first.)

Additional Eulogy Details:

There are three styles to eulogies:

Thematic Stories: More poetic, more story-focused, this style is especially helpful when there are big gaps that the family cannot (or will not) fill in. I look for a theme (Mary approached life like a puzzle...; Everyone who knew Bob will have a funny story to tell ...). It's not always obvious, but there is typically a thread that weaves it all together. I use this in the service as a whole, but especially for the coherence of a eulogy. Family members or friends might each want to speak to different themes, rather than time periods.

Chronological: from birth to death – highlights / details / who, what, when, where, why / similar to a résumé format (but less technical, of course!) If family is doing the eulogy in the thematic style, I will work some of these details into my parts of the service, so they are not missed.

Blend: Most eulogies are a blend. Highlights of the chronology, embellishing on the themes that emerge. I ensure that I have a chronology of their whole life, checking for gaps. What about the 1950s and 60s – where were they then? What are the essential details that _____ would want shared?

You can never perfectly capture someone's life in just a few minutes. The eulogy is simply an invitation. I share the highlights of someone's life, honoring their journey. The aim is to inspire others: to remember their own stories; to reflect on their own experiences; to share them at the reception; to begin or continue their process of letting go.

When you know, or suspect, that there is a secret ... or a problem ...

(Complicated relationships / suicide that is not named / violence / etc.)

First, I reassure the family that I will not embarrass them, or put them on the spot. Secondly, I encourage them to tell me the story, as much as they are comfortable.

"I understand that your loved one was a challenging (complicated / powerful / strong willed…) person. Let's find a way to remember them – without putting you in an uncomfortable position, but also without saying things that weren't true. We can be honest and discreet."

"I see this is an especially painful time for you. We don't want to make that any harder. We will be careful, together, to be honest but not voyeuristic."

"I would like to understand ____'s story. Anything you say that you don't want repeated, don't hesitate to tell me. I'll mark it as 'private', and it will just be in my notes so that I understand the bigger picture."

Sometimes I know the story but the family isn't talking. Sometimes I don't know the story but I am picking up 'gaps' or discomfort. I might offer a suggestion like:

"How about if I say "____ was a complicated person. They wanted the best for everyone, but that goal was sometimes out of reach."

Or "____had a hard time making their way in the world."

Discreet truths are a great relief for the crowd, who usually know or suspect.

A note about religious input, intentional or accidental:

Sometimes, for a ceremony to serve the whole family, there will be people who bring religious elements to the table. The memorial might be for a humanist, while the deceased's spouse, child or parent is religious. Or, the organizers might be humanist, but the deceased held a religious or spiritual perspective on life. Organizers may ask for help with this, while remaining true to a humanist service. There are three ways I deal with this:

If the organizers are not interested in including a religious or spiritual element, I reassure them that this is their service to design and that it should be true to the deceased – to those who are at the heart of the celebration. People are often afraid of disappointing their loved ones and may need your support in making this decision. You have to be especially careful about 'open microphones' in this case, because you cannot control unscripted speakers.

If they remain concerned about their religious relatives or friends, but want to preserve the humanist service, I encourage them to think about ways they might give space to those folks at the reception. Are they comfortable with an open mic at the reception? Or someone saying a blessing before the meal?

If the organizers decide they need to include religious or spiritual elements in the service, then I introduce them saying some-

thing like: "For those of you with Christian roots, we will now read ...." Or, "Because it is important to the extended family, we offer this reading ...." Or, "This was _____'s favorite poem/song/scripture passage...." Alternately, the organizers might invite the religious person to do the reading. With all of these ways, the humanist integrity of the service and/or speaker is protected, because we have politely, respectfully distanced ourselves from the belief, while including an element that was determined to be important.

The Elements of a Funeral/Memorial Service

Humanist funerals and memorials, like humanist weddings, are quite flexible and can include an unknown variety of elements. The traditional funeral, however has the following elements:

- Welcome/Opening Words
- Eulogy
- Memories
- Songs, poetry, etc.
- Moment of Silence
- Closing Words

Again, we'll use this traditional formula to help you get the hang of writing a funeral or memorial service. Once you're comfortable writing and conducting a service, you can then add new elements.

Welcome/Opening Words

As the celebrant, you will be welcoming guests to the service and setting the tone. Always remember that you are facilitating an experience of mourning and refrain from "humanist evangelizing" or in any way including your own views or advice except where they coincide with the family's wishes. Most of all, please do not criticize traditional religion. Most likely there will be religious friends and family at the service who are only there to mourn and celebrate in the way that is appropriate for them.

That said, your opening words can be a great place to say a few words about humanism's views on living and dying, if they are appropriate. Again, always consult the family first. As mentioned earlier, I think humanist philosophy has much to offer those that are grieving. Rather than offering sentiments such as "she's in a better place" or "you'll see him in heaven" (statements that bother many traditionally religious people as well as the nonreligious!) you have a chance to help your guests reflect on what makes for a good life and what effect good living can have on succeeding generations.

Begin your opening words by introducing yourself as a humanist celebrant and explaining why you are all gathered here. It is important that you mention the name of the deceased often because they are the center of the celebration. After any general or humanist thoughts about life and death, you will want to give an overview of their life. This can be very short, about the length of an obituary, or longer if the family wishes it. You don't want to get too in depth and take away from the coming eulogy or stories the family might wish to share themselves. In my opinion, it is always a good idea to end by expressing gratitude toward the family to be given the opportunity of celebrating the life of their loved one.

Eulogy and Memories

One of the most moving parts of any funeral or memorial is when people share memories and funny stories in an open mic format. However, it is always a good idea to have someone also deliver a formal eulogy. I think this is best done before any open mic speaking as it gives us a sense of the life of the deceased and allows the stories that follow to elaborate with details and also be more casual. Sharing memories after the eulogy also gives people a moment of lightness after the emotional rollercoaster that often accompanies a eulogy. When the service is pre-planned, the client may wish to designate a specific individual to give the eulogy, otherwise, the family will likely choose someone. Be prepared to do the eulogy yourself either in the case that you are chosen or if the person chosen breaks down and can't continue. For timing purposes, the eulogy should be no longer than ten minutes. If it goes longer, don't interrupt to shorten it. If you're using a rented space and need to be out by a designated time, just shorten another part of the service. A tactful way to make sure things run smoothly and on time is to suggest a specific amount of time to the eulogist during consultation.

It may so happen that the person who has died was difficult or that it can be hard to write a eulogy full of fond memories. While you never want to "speak ill of the dead", it is okay to mention a few human failings by giving them a positive twist such as, "Jeremy could be rough with people with whom he disagreed but he was a doting father to Jenny." See Anne Barker's tips listed above for dealing with these kinds of situations.

After the eulogy, it is a good idea to ask immediate family to make any statements, tell any stories that they wish and only then move on to the open mic, if the family has requested one. Though you certainly don't want to tell anyone that their time is up, make it clear in the program that you are allotting a certain amount of time for this activity. A funeral or memorial should be about the same length as a traditional church service or shorter. It is always a good idea to ask a family member to close the period of sharing with a word of thanks and perhaps a few more words about their loved one.

Other Elements

Other elements of a good funeral or memorial service include music, a moment of silence, readings, and personal rituals.

Music

At the very least, it is good to have music as guests enter and depart the ceremony but your clients may also wish for musical interludes. This might include selections played by family members and friends or it can be as lighthearted as a singalong. Make sure you are in contact with any musicians and that you have any CDs, MP3s, or other necessary items prior to the ceremony. ALWAYS do a mic/sound system check before guests arrive and make sure your audio files or CDs are of decent quality.

There are no rules about what kind of music you can have at a funeral or memorial service. Most of this will depend on the wishes of the family. However, remember that the music you play as guests enter and leave sets a tone. You may want to have more reflective music playing as guests enter and something slightly more lighthearted to send them away. Begin playing music approximately five minutes before guests arrive. Exit music should play for five minutes after guests begin to depart.

Moment of Silence

Traditionally religious funerals have many prayers but as nontheists we often substitute that with a moment of silence. This allows any religious guests to offer silent prayer as well as nontheistic guests to have a moment of meditation and/or reflection. I always think this element goes well after the eulogy as it gives guests a moment to collect their thoughts before sharing their own memories and stories. One to two minutes is sufficient.

Readings

Many funerals and memorials include readings such as a favorite poem or story or even just a quote. Make sure you find out if this is an element your clients want to include. It makes a great transition between speakers and is a wonderful way for family members to participate. There are many great resources available for readings. A. C. Grayling's *The Humanist Bible* and Humanists UK's (formerly the British Humanist Association's) *Funerals Without God* by Jane Wynne Willson are just two noteworthy examples.

Other Rituals

Your client may have requested that other rituals be added to the service. In some cases, the client knows exactly what they want but in most cases, they will only know that they want something meaningful that will add beauty and warmth to the ceremony. Here are some examples that you might suggest to undecided clients:

- A slideshow of happy and meaningful moments
- Seeds for guests to take home and plant in remembrance
- A memory book for guests to write in and which can be presented to the family
- Releasing doves, balloons, or lanterns
- Signing the casket (for very lighthearted funerals)
- Raising a glass

The Day of the Service

Before you even leave the house, make sure you are wearing something appropriate both for the occasion and your role. Not very many people dress in black for funerals and memorials anymore but, just like with my advice for weddings, you don't want to be the center of attention either. My suggestion is that, unless requested otherwise, you should wear either black or darker colors such as gray or dark blue. If you wear makeup, try to refrain from putting on that new bright blue nail polish with the sparkles that you love. If you wear a tie, make sure it is not too loud. While you don't want to create a depressing atmosphere, you should keep it reflective and professional. Again, this advice may not apply to all settings and circumstances. Also, before you leave the house, make sure you have at least two copies of the ceremony script and any music you may need as well as other items and equipment.

Just like with a wedding, you'll want to arrive at least an hour early to make sure everything is arranged. Do a last-minute mic/sound system check. Make sure you have everything you need and if you are using a funeral home, be sure you introduce yourself to the director if you have not met them already. It is also a good idea to make sure that the seats at the front of the venue have been reserved for family and close friends.

Stop by the room that is usually set up for the family to offer your condolences (even if you have done this during a consultation). Ask them if they have any questions and run through the order of service one last time. When everyone is ready, you can lead the family into the service and seat them at the front unless other arrangements have been made. You can then take your place and begin the celebration. If there is to be a reception to follow, make sure you let the guests know at the end of the service. Before you leave, remember to step down, shake hands with the family and thank them for allowing you to share in their moment.

Pro Tip

When it comes to your ceremony script, it is a good idea to print it out in a font slightly larger than you normally would. You will want to be making frequent eye contact with the guests as you speak and having your script in larger font will make it harder to lose your spot in the text.

Also, if the funeral or memorial is being held outdoors, remember to slide the script into sets of plastic cover sheets. You never know what the weather may be like! In fact, don't forget an umbrella as well!

Sometimes family members like to have copies of the script. For this, you will want to readjust the font and make sure you do a thorough read-through to catch any typos or misspellings. Many people like to have this little memento, especially if they were very emotional during the service and can't remember just what was said.

What If Think I Might Cry?

Anne Barker, a Unitarian Universalist minister and my good friend, is a pro at doing funeral/memorial services. When I asked her what advice she'd give to someone nervous about performing one, she wrote the following:

How to Keep from Crying

1. Practice your words ahead of time, out loud. Read them aloud, again and again, until you can read them through without your voice shaking. Having a muscle memory of 'getting through it' will go a long way on the day.

2. Take a moment for a deep breath or three. It may seem like for-ever to you, but it will really only be a few seconds, most people won't even notice, and if they do they will understand.

3. Take a sip of water. (I always have water at the front, for this rea-son.)

4. If you feel your voice starting to crack, drop it lower. We go higher when we get nervous, and going higher makes you more likely to lose control. Dropping your voice lower will instantly help you to improve control.

5. Don't look at the people who are crying. Lock eyes with a crying Mama, and you're a goner! Cast a soft glance 'over the crowd' but

not directly into their eyes, and it will be much easier.

6. Most importantly, it's ok to be emotional. This can be a time of big feelings. Don't be hard on yourself – just take a breath, have a sip of water and/or lower your voice … and carry on when you are ready.

My voice cracks a tiny bit in most services – at the wedding pronouncement, or when I say something tender like "Mary has died." It can be a very moving experience. When my feelings start to rise – especially if I am marrying friends, or burying a loved one – I say to myself, "I am here to help these people. Right now, this is not about me." Then I take a breath, or a sip of water, drop my voice lower and carry on.

If the service is for someone especially close to me, or when I was just starting out, I would read the whole service aloud, again, the morning of the event. Then, if I needed to, I had time to cry … and to pull myself back together. Feelings are nothing to be ashamed of. We just need to learn how to manage them.

Bonus Tip: If I am tired, it is way harder to not cry. A good sleep makes a huge difference.

The Difficult Ones: Suicide and the Death of a Child

Every death is tragic to someone, somewhere. Everyone who dies leaves behind family, friends, caretakers. The death of a ninety-three-year-old woman is no less a loss than the death of a child. A natural death is no less a loss than a suicide. And yet, the death of a child or the death of someone by suicide does add new dimensions to our grief and they can be especially difficult for celebrants to deal with. What do we say that doesn't sound trite to the parents who have just lost a small child? How can we comfort the friends and family of someone who died by suicide?

I firmly believe that we can't. That is to say that we can offer small comforts in the gift of a sensitive and moving service but we ultimately must let go of the idea that anything we say or do will change the horrific reality that these friends and family must endure. If we can focus on creating as personal and touching a ceremony as we can, we can more easily take on the task and we will have fulfilled our purpose.

But what do we actually do? How are the "difficult ones" different in practice?

The Death of a Child

Without a doubt, losing a child is the most horrible thing a parent can imagine. The bond between a parent and child is so profound there are few words to describe it. To lose a child is very much like losing a part of yourself. Because the loss is so great, any celebrant taking on the job of doing a service for a child must remember that the wishes of the parents absolutely come before anything else. This funeral or memorial is entirely for them.

Consulting with grieving parents can be very hard. Because funerals and memorials take place so closely following death, the parents will sometimes still be in shock, even if the death was expected. Their emotions will be raw and they may have difficulty communicating their wishes. In some cases, they may be in denial. This can make it hard to get all the information you need to do the service. However, if you approach the consultation with sensitivity, not handing out platitudes but simply acknowledging the grief that exists, you can create a meaningful service for their child.

As with any funeral or memorial consultation, begin by offering your condolences. Don't pretend you understand this loss unless you yourself have lost a child. Don't try to compare their loss with a different one you have suffered in an attempt to forge a connection. Just allow that grief to be present and to be expressed. Take your time with this consultation. Allow the parents to speak on their own terms. It may help to ask for a photo of the child. Look at it together and ask them about him or her. Aside from the standard questions, ask what the pregnancy was like, what birth was like. What was it like the first time their child smiled? Do they remember the first day of school? When the child lost their first tooth? What was their first Halloween costume? Asking these questions allows the parents to relive happy memories while also giving you a sense of this family's life together and what the child meant to them. However, be prepared. Some parents may not want to answer some of these questions. It might be too hard for them to think about.

When it comes to the specifics of a funeral or memorial for a child, little details make a great difference. For instance, generally celebrants or officiants will not call it a funeral but a celebration of life. This is because the child's death is already traumatic enough and what most people will want to do is to remember the happy moments. Renaming it a celebration of life allows people to properly grieve while also highlighting the importance of the brief life of that child.

Music and reading selections might also be different. Though, of course, you will want to respect the wishes of the parents, generally speaking, most children's services don't have dramatic or mournful music and readings. Instead, consider using songs that the child liked. As for readings, a favorite child's poem or story can be very touching.

Some celebrants are understandingly concerned about what to say when it comes to the opening words. For instance, how much do we talk about how tragic it is to lose a child? In general, unless specifically advised not to do so, it is okay to give expression to what everyone in that room is feeling – traumatic loss. However, keep these thoughts confined to the opening words. Everyone will want to concentrate only on the child's life when it comes to the other elements of the ceremony.

Suicide

Like the loss of a child, the loss of a loved one by suicide is shocking and often seems senseless. We struggle to understand what happened, what we could have done. We look for signs we may have missed or we feel guilty about our relationship with that person. When dealing with funerals and memorials for those who have committed suicide, the celebrant is actually dealing with a much larger group of traumatized people.

Much of the same advice given in the last section applies here as well. Consultations with survivors should be sensitive. If you have any biases about mental illness, you need to deal with them before taking on this work. In fact, if you plan to offer funeral and memorial services at all, my suggestion is that you become very familiar with the realities of mental illness and suicide and also the affects these have on survivors. The last thing you want to do is to go into a consultation and say the wrong thing. There are many, many books out there written with survivors in mind, such as *No Time to Say Goodbye:Surviving the Suicide of a Loved One* by Carla Fine and *I Wasn't Ready to Say Goodbye: Surviving, Coping, and Healing After the Sudden Death of a Loved One* by Brook Noel and Pamela Blair that I think are worthwhile reading for any celebrant.

When it comes to your opening words, be careful what you say. You should ask during consultation whether it is generally known that their loved one took their own life. It's not unusual for families to not want suicide mentioned either because it is not generally known or because it is simply their wish. If they do want to be open about it, you should too. Without dwelling on it, you can mention the manner of death by emphasizing that the deceased was a sensitive person who sometimes found it hard to cope. Again, as with ceremonies dealing with the death of children, you will probably want to confine these kinds of statements to your opening words so that the rest of the service can focus on the positive life of the loved one.

Funerals and memorials are the hardest work that we do. They can be emotionally devastating, such as when dealing with suicide or children, and it can be hard to be witness to so much grief time after time. And yet, difficult as they are, they are sometimes our most rewarding work. As more people search for secular alternatives to religious funerals, we can step up and provide peace of mind, assuring families and friends that we will conduct a service as true to their loved one as possible. I hope that this chapter provided you with enough tips and advice to make you a little less nervous about offering this valuable service to your community.

Example Funeral and Memorial Services

Ian Bushfield, Humanist Officiant and Executive Director of the British Columbia Humanist Association

Opening Words

We have gathered here this morning to mark the death and honor to the character of Sarah Jane Brookings who died on June 5th at the age of 93. In keeping with Sarah's view of life, I have been invited here as an Officiant of the British Columbia Humanist Association to speak for the human community of which she was part.

Death is a very personal matter for those who know it in someone close to them. But we are all concerned, directly or indirectly, with the death of any individual, for we are all members of one human community, and no one of us is independent and separate. Though some of the links are strong and some are tenuous, each of us is joined to all others by links of kinship, love, friendship, or by living in the same neighborhood or town or country, or simply by our own common humanity.

No one should be afraid of death itself: it is as natural as life. Only nature is permanent. All that has life has its beginning and its end…and life exists in the time span between birth and death. For those of us who do not have a religious faith, and who believe that death brings the end of individual existence, life's significance lies in the experiences and the satisfactions we achieve in that span of time; its permanence lies in the memories of those who knew us, and any influence we have left behind.

The atoms that made up Sarah's body were forged in the furnaces of stars millions and billions of years ago. Today we release those atoms back to the universe to fuel new lives and new stories. Sarah's life has come to an end but she continues on, less orderly than before. Her life is given meaning by our memories and the never-ending cycle of nature.

So, we should be daring enough to remember Sarah with happiness. Sarah cared passionately about others, loving her late brother most of all. She often went out of her way to help those in need. She empathized strongly with animals, demonstrating her deep personal connection to the natural world. Let us remember her compassion, her empathy, her art, and her love. I ask that we take a moment to reflect – and for those who choose to offer a silent prayer – on one of Sarah's favorite poems, The Nature of Things, by the Roman poet and Epicurean philosopher Lucretius:

"No single thing abides; but all things flow.
Fragment to fragment clings - the things thus grow
Until we know and name them. By degrees
They melt, and are no more the things we know.
Globed from the atoms falling slow or swift"
"I see the suns, I see the systems lift
Their forms; and even the systems and the suns
Shall go back slowly to the eternal drift.
You too, oh earth - your empires, lands, and seas -
Least with your stars, of all the galaxies,
Globed from the drift like these, like these you too
Shalt go. You are going, hour by hour, like these.
Nothing abides. The seas in delicate haze
Go off; those mooned sands forsake their place;
And where they are, shall other seas in turn

Mow with their scythes of whiteness other bays.

The seeds that once were we take flight and fly,

Winnowed to earth, or whirled along the sky,

Not lost but disunited. Life lives on.

It is the lives, the lives, the lives, that die.

They go beyond recapture and recall,

Lost in the all-indissoluble All;

Gone like the rainbow from the fountain's foam,

Gone like the spindrift shuddering down the squall.

Flakes of the water, on the waters cease!

Soul of the body, melt and sleep like these.

Atoms to atoms - weariness to rest -

Ashes to ashes - hopes and fears to peace!

O Science, lift aloud your voice that stills

The pulse of fear, and through the conscience thrills -

Thrills through the conscience with the news of peace -

How beautiful your feet are on the hills!"

[Minute of silence]

The Tribute

[Music fades back in, start slideshow]

Sarah lived a long life filled with many happy memories of her brother and her art. Born in England, Sarah grew up and remained very close with her mother and brother Robert throughout their lives. A free spirit, but not a trouble maker, Sarah completed high school and went on to pursue her passion for art in post-secondary education.

And it is that art for which Sarah will perhaps be most remembered. An extraordinary artist, Sarah excelled at every form she attempted, particularly her beautiful calligraphy. For the Queen's coronation, Sarah was commissioned by the government to create a leather-bound copy of the Rubaiyat of Omar Khayyam. This and other examples of her work are on display here today.

From a young age, Sarah's family instilled in her a compassion and kindness that she maintained throughout her long life. One of her first memories was of standing on the side of the road as a horse carried buggy went by with a little girl in it about four years old. The little girl had a band around her arm, which Sarah didn't know what meant. Another girl was standing with Sarah on the side of the road and she put up her hand and pointed all of her fingers at the little girl, and started shouting names at her. Sarah recalled running home to tell her father what had happened. He sat her on his lap, hugged her, and explained that the girl in the buggy was Jewish, and that the other little girl had learned to be hateful from her parents. He went on to explain why we should all love each other regardless of what we believe, or what we look like. It wasn't so much what her father had said that impressed upon her so much, as how he said it. Sarah remembered the desperation in his voice, almost like he was begging her to understand how important compassion was.

Sarah's empathy led her to abhor injustice of all kinds. She recognized that judging people on the color of their skin was wrong at a time when Canada charged a head tax on Asian immigrants. In fact one of her first boyfriends over eighty years ago was Chinese.

Sarah also deplored homophobia and cruelty toward animals. Jamie described Sarah's love of animals to me as "almost to the point of irrationality." She had an overabundance of cats and dogs in her life. One time, Sarah stole a baby duck from the bird sanctuary because geese were picking on it. Sarah raised it in her own home until she set it free in her pond. Sarah dated and loved various men, but she never married, fearing that by doing so, she would lose her independence. Above all else though, Sarah's deepest love was for her brother Robert. Together they owned a store in Cape Breton and that is where Sarah's ashes will be taken after today, so that they may be reunited once more.

I would now like to invite Carolyn, Robert's daughter, to read one of Robert's poems in Sarah's honor.

[Robert's poem read by Carolyn]

The Committal

Will you please stand for the committal? Here, in this last act, immune now to the changes and chances of our mortal lot, we commit the body of Sarah Jane Brookings to its natural end.

(Music plays)

Closing Words

Please be seated.

I want to thank you all for allowing me to share this moment with you. It saddens me to have not had the chance to meet Sarah during her life, only getting to know her through stories told to me second hand from her friends. It is through these stories though that Sarah will live on. Take her with you on your journeys through life.

In sadness for her death but with appreciation for her life, we choose to remember Sarah and her talent for art and her passion for life. Finally, as we leave to continue our own voyage of discovery in the world, let us remember the following passages of The Rubaiyat of Omar Khayyam as a reminder of our own mortality and to make the most of what time we have.

> The bird of life is singing in the sun,
> Short is his song, nor only just begun,—
> A call, a trill, a rapture, then—so soon!—
> A silence, and the song is done—is done.
> Would you be happy! hearken, then, the way:
> Heed not To-morrow, heed not Yesterday;
> The magic words of life are Here and Now—
> O fools, that after some to-morrow stray!
> To all of us the thought of heaven is dear—

Why not be sure of it and make it here?

No doubt there is a heaven yonder too,

But 'tis so far away—and you are near.

Look not above, there is no answer there;

Pray not, for no one listens to your prayer;

Near is as near to God as any Far,

And Here is just the same deceit as There.

Ah, make the most of what we may yet spend,

Before we too into the Dust descend;

Dust into Dust, and under Dust, to lie;

Sans Wine, sans Song, sans Singer, and – sans End!

For some we loved, the loveliest and best

That from His rolling vintage Time has pressed,

Have drunk their glass a round or two before,

And one by one crept silently to rest.

Kenna Covington of North Carolina Secular Weddings

Can we please join hands to show our love for N.

It's the same story the crow told me

It's the only one he knows –
like the morning sun you come
and like the wind you go.
Thank you.

Good evening. My name is Kenna Covington and I am honored to be with you as we have gathered to mourn the death and celebrate the life of N.

N's family would like to thank you all for being here – at a place none of us could have imagined a week ago. Your support, your love, and your kindness are legendary. The world has lost a light, a very bright light. He passed away on Saturday and his sudden death has left a very large, N-sized hole in all of us. We are sad. We have questions. We are grieving. And we are feeling these things together.

Tonight, we are joined in our sadness. This sadness will take many forms and may never leave us, but as in life – and the life N lived, there is balance – so we'll take tonight to remember the love, the kindness, the compassion, and joy that was N, the gentle giant who made friends wherever he went; someone who saw the best in others and brought out the best in in all of us.

Take a moment, if you can – and look to the people around you. Go ahead. What we recognize in each other is not only the same pain and bewilderment, but something more – your shared experiences with N. These are memories of good times, close times, silly jokes, and laughter. Many of you may not know each other here tonight because N's friends were as eclectic as his taste in music, but what we see in each other, what brings us together tonight is that we were all lucky enough to know and love him – and we carry him with us.

I didn't know N personally, but I know I wish I had. He was a bright, artistic guy who felt a real connection with humanity. R and C told me that he was a fun kid to raise – that everything was magical for N – that as a little boy, he was so amazed and excited for many things people take for granted such as frost on the grass in the mornings. His fascination with people, animals, and the natural world were expressed in his compassion and kind nature. His love and friendship with his best friend, his brother, J, was something most parents only wish for their children. Love came naturally to N – feeling it and sharing it.

At first glance, N was a big, burly guy, the kind of figure you don't want to mess with – but then there's this big, burly guy wearing a bright pink polo or his favorite tie-dyed shirt and your brain does a little train wreck thing. There's so much more to this guy than meets the eye.

N had so many interests and loves. At the top of this list is music. He was part of the Marching Spartans at S High School, where he played the French horn. He also could play the guitar and trumpet. He loved food, particularly limes – if you were looking for him, just follow the trail of lime peels until you found him. N was a free spirit who followed his own path.

While N was a wrestler in high-school, he didn't have a mean bone in his body. In fact, in all of his matches, he only won one. And instead of being boastful and self-aggrandizing, he felt horrible for the other guy. This is N – always thinking of others and looking for ways to help and make their lives better.

N was a honey badger when it came to his appearance. He didn't need outside validation for how he looked. He was comfortable wearing what made him happy – from his bright green shoes to his dancing bears shirts. N was more concerned with being connected with what was on the inside than he was about impressing people with what was on the outside. That's pretty cool – and it was never a show – just genuine N, the genuine, gentle giant.

We all get excited when we meet someone who expresses on their outside the things we like about ourselves on the inside - this is how I think N made friends. He was a bit shy at first, but once he opened up, he was an unending fountain of love and kindness. There was never any judgment. No discrimination. No hate. It was all peace and love – he was a very good hippie. N took the time to get to know you and it didn't matter if you were religious or not, the color of your skin, or how far you made it in school. He was love - and accepted you on a level that not many people are capable of. He made friends for life, deep, rich connections – and this is why you all had so much trouble finding parking tonight.

Part of what makes this so tough is that he was one of the best people many of us will ever know. Tonight, we honor and remember N with our love and our acceptance – and shine our light for him, because like Jerry said: I ain't often right, but I've never been wrong. It seldom turns out the way it does in the song. Once in awhile you get shown the light – in the strangest of places if you look at it right.

R is one of N's best friends and he is going to play a couple of songs for N and for us.

[R plays music]

Thank you, R. That was beautiful. And now, N's friend, K is going to share a poem with us.

[K reads poem]

Thank you, K. NW is a family friend and will share the eulogy created by N's family.

[NW delivers eulogy]

Thank you, NW

No one person can sum up the life of another. It takes all of us – what we share is a mosaic – happy thoughts and warm memories, mixed with sadness for our loss. This is a time of openness, sharing, and celebration. And while sharing right now may be too difficult for you, it's alright – we know your hearts are full of love for N. The floor is open, and, as you feel moved to, you can come up to the podium if you like, or stand where you are if you are more comfortable – and share your favorite N memory.

[Guests share stories]

Thank you for sharing your memories and great stories with us. N really was one of the best people any of us will ever meet – and we are all better for knowing him.

There really is no way to wrap our heads around his death. We'll be thinking about him for the rest of our days. In our own ways we will grieve. Were he here, he'd give us all hugs and tell us not to worry, that everything will be alright – and remind us that Albus Dumbledore taught us that the pain we all feel at this dreadful loss reminds me, reminds us, that while we may come from different places and speak in different tongues, our hearts beat as one. To be so young at his death is certainly a tragedy, but it may be the equal balance to the brightness of his being. The image I have of N is of the yin and yang symbol. Where there is shadow, there is also light – and we need the contrast of each one to see the other. N's light shined so brightly that it helped the rest of us see more clearly.

As we leave here tonight and return to our homes, you carry N's light with you. Remember the yin and the yang – that there is positive and negative in all of us and in every situation - and if you can turn one negative thing in your life into a positive, then you are sharing N's light with the world and his memory remains alive. The whole thing is remembering, this is who we are. Let love define you, not your mistakes. And if you get confused, just listen to the music play. We remember N and celebrate what a long strange trip it's been.

Peace.

Funeral/Memorial Element Idea

Frank Harlan, humanist celebrant, Seattle, Washington

When I am hosting a Celebration of Life Memorial I know there are a lot of folks that are afraid of public speaking and would be way too uncomfortable standing in front of the guests to speak. So, what I like to do, to give others a chance to share their feelings, is to hand out a sheet of paper with three questions on it. I do this as guest are arriving and request that any guest, who would like to, consider answering one of the questions … only one. Then I collect the questionnaires and sort into piles by Questions 1, 2 and 3 before the ceremony.

Three Questions about (Deceased's Full Name)

Your Name:_____

1. How did you know when (Deceased's First Name) was Happy?
2. Something you loved, admired and/or adored about (Deceased's First Name).
3. Would you like to share a story about (Deceased's First Name) with everyone?

If so, write your name and your relationship to (Deceased's First Name).

Remember to have several ink pens and to leave lots of space between questions for guests to write their answer. I usually add three to four lines below each question for them to write on. The way I incorporate the answers is that I read six to ten from questions #1 or #2 between outros and intros of guest speakers. I start off by introducing the question and then reading aloud the person's name and what they wrote. Question #3 I save for last (usually prior to the slide show), and instead of inviting the people who have requested to share a story to come to the podium, I walk the microphone to them and let them stand and speak from the where they are seated, or have them step out into the aisle.

CHAPTER 5

Other Humanist Ceremonies

More than likely you will be called on to do weddings and memorial services. But that shouldn't stop you from offering a variety of ceremony options to your community. Any special event or occasion can be turned into a ceremony from a baby naming to a trans naming. There are also vow renewals, invocations, seasonal changes, and so much more. In the following chapter, I will address all of these different types of ceremonies and leave you with a few sample ceremonies to get the creative juices flowing.

Baby Naming

Some of us may not be big on baptism but many of us DO like to welcome in the little ones! Luckily for humanists we have baby namings! These ceremonies allow us to welcome our babies not just to life but into the communities that mean the most to us. For some of us, that may be family and friends while others might want to include their local humanist and freethought groups or nontheistic churches. In whatever context or location, it's a great excuse for a party! Baby naming ceremonies are quite common across religions as well as cultures and secular communities. There has always been significance associated with an individual's name. For secular people, it can be as simple as an acknowledgement of the preciousness and promise of each and every one of us.

Consultation

As always, you should meet with the parent(s) of the child in advance of the ceremony so that you can create something meaningful together. Questions to ask include the child's name, names of parents and guideparents (an alternative to godparents, if desired), what sort of tone they are looking for, number of guests, whether anyone else will be participating, whether there are any rituals or family traditions they'd like included, etc. You will also want to send your client(s) away with some homework - to think about and write down what it is that they want to say for the parents' promise section.

Many people wonder about how much to charge clients for this kind of ceremony or even whether to charge them at all. As always, this is a personal preference. Some celebrants offer free or reduced prices to members of their humanist communities while others ask simply for a donation. Still others will charge a full price for everyone. It's always a good idea when setting your price structure to check out the websites of celebrants in your area to see what they do. Generally speaking, when it comes to prices, most celebrants charge between $100-$200 for this ceremony. Whether you decide to charge or not, remember that your work and your time are valuable, especially because you're creating entirely original ceremonies. Don't be afraid to charge what you're worth. People are more than happy to pay for a moving and memorable ceremony.

Writing the Ceremony

Below are the basic elements of a baby naming ceremony. Remember that you don't have to follow this order or even include all of these elements. This just gives a starting place to begin thinking about how to write a ceremony. You can also include other ritual elements such as poetry, music, and, if you belong to secular Judaism or practice other nontheistic religions, cultural observances that reflect those values and beliefs.

The basic features of a baby naming ceremony are:

- Welcome/Opening Words
- Giving the Name
- Parents' Promise
- Guideparents and Guideparents' Promises
- Presentation of the Child
- Closing Words

Opening Words/Welcome

Like the wedding and the funeral/memorial, you begin by welcoming everyone and explaining why they're here. This is also a good moment to say a few words about the importance of new life to that community. You want your opening words to set the tone, whether this is a solemn ceremony, a humorous one, formal, or informal. Match your words to the occasion and also remember that many attendees may not have ever participated in either a baptism or a baby naming ceremony. Your opening words should help put people at ease and give them a sense of why you are all gathered as well as what is expected of them.

Giving the Name

This is the actual moment when you or the parent(s) officially name the child. It is likely that everyone already knows the name but this is also a good place for family to talk about the significance of the name, its history, its cultural meaning, or they can talk about ancestors with this name. This particular element can be placed either at the beginning of the ceremony as I have done here, or at the end to function as a climax before sending guests away.

Parents' Promise

This is where the parent(s) speak directly to their child the promises they make to them. This can be written personally by the parent(s) or the celebrant may be asked to draft something for them. Obviously, if you're being asked to draft it, make sure to ask the parent(s) what they most wish for the child. You don't want to write in something generic. Think about the promises as you would wedding vows. Parents might promise support, love, understanding, and all the same things you find in a wedding vow. However, for a humorous ceremony parents might also want to sneak in a few funny promises as well. Always consider the overall tone of the ceremony when writing or helping your clients to write their promises.

Selection of Guideparent(s) and Their Promises

While baptisms have godparents, humanist baby namings have guideparents! Guideparents are one or more individuals chosen to be the child's mentors throughout life. In some cases, guideparents, like godparents, also promise to care for the children in the event of their parents' deaths. If your clients wish to include guideparents, ensure that they clearly communicate to both you and those selected exactly what this role entails ahead of time so that there is no confusion.

Like the parents' promise, the guideparents' promises can be personal or the words of the celebrant but they should always be mindful of the agreed upon role that the guideparents will play.

Presentation of the Child

The presentation of the child, like all of these ceremonial elements, can be moved around to suit the flow of the ceremony you write. For instance, it can be paired with giving the name or it can be part of your closing words. How you determine the best fit is up to you and your clients. The presentation is simply when the celebrant presents the child to the community, calling them by their full name and saying a few words to the child about their role in the community gathered.

Closing Words

You can then close with a few short words. These can be just about anything that gives the community a new sense of cohesion and appreciation for the new life among them.

Example Baby Naming

"This naming ceremony was performed for a couple that wanted to introduce their new daughter to their humanist community using a brief but meaningful ceremony." – Autumn Reinhardt-Simpson, Edmonton, Alberta

Welcome and Opening Words

Celebrant: "Welcome, friends and family, to the Thompson home. Thank you for being here to support them as they welcome their newest family member. My name is _____ and I am a humanist celebrant endorsed by the Humanist Society. As humanists themselves the Thompsons asked me to perform this ceremony and I am honored to do so.

New life brings with it so much promise as well as anxiety! We don't yet know what triumphs and disappointments this child will experience. We plan, we worry, and we hope for the best. But one of the greatest moments of welcoming new life is recognizing the opportunity we all have as friends, family, and community, to help shape a child's experience. We have the chance to ensure that not only is this child brought up to be compassionate and thoughtful, within a loving community, but we also have the opportunity to see our shared community grow stronger with the infusion of new energy and new ideas. The new life in this family brings with it renewed life to our community.

And so, just as parents are responsible for the care and education of this new child, so are we all being asked to support the Thompsons as they undertake this incredible task of rearing a new human being.

Giving the Name

Celebrant: "Friends and family, it is my honor to introduce to you the newest member of this community, Helen Jane Thompson. Helen means "shining light" and her parents hope that this is what Helen will be to all who know her."

"May she be a beacon of compassion seen from a lonely plain."

"May she light the way for those who turn to her in their troubles."

"May she discover the shining light within herself."

Parents' Promise

Celebrant: "Many people see promises as a binding vow that will never be broken. And when a promise is broken, even unintentionally, we tend to think that the one who promised us did so in bad faith. However, perhaps the better way to look at a promise is that it isn't a perfect statement of who we are, but rather of what we strive to be. As parents, we all do the best we can. We sometimes start with the best of intentions only to find ourselves coming up short. But this should never make us jaded or unwilling to make promises and it shouldn't make us unwilling to accept promises from others. From now on, let's view a promise as something less than perfect, as the innermost striving of one very imperfect human heart to another.

"Alan and Jenny would now like to share their promises with Helen."

(Parents give their promises)

Guideparents

Celebrant: "Because raising a human being is a communal process, Alan and Jenny have chosen Seth and Karen to be Helen's guideparents.

"Seth and Karen, you are being asked to fulfil the role of mentor to this new child as she navigates life and creates her purpose. Please step forward and share the promises you've written to her."

(Guideparents give their promises)

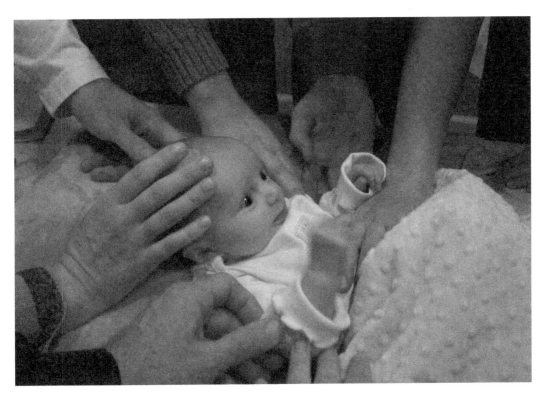

This was a naming/welcoming ceremony for a new baby girl to the Gould family.

Presentation of the Child

Celebrant: "Family and friends, I present to you the newest member of our humanist community, Helen Jane Thompson."

Closing Words

Celebrant: Alan and Jenny would like to thank everyone for coming today. Your presence here is proof of your support and love during this new phase of their life. May we all grow together and deepen our commitment to one another as we work together to raise this precious new gift.

Name Day Ceremony by Victoria Gipson

Introduction and Welcome

Celebrant: Good afternoon and welcome to you all! I am Victoria Gipson, a humanist celebrant trained and endorsed by the Humanist Society an adjunct of the American Humanist Association.

Today Michelle & Jourdan invited you here to celebrate with them, because you are the most important people in their child's life and you will be instrumental in helping Olli discover his place in the family, and the wider community of the world we live in. Michelle & Jourdan believe it is important to have this gathering to welcome Olli, surround him with the people who have been a part of the unfolding adventure of their lives, and ask you to play a part in their child's new life as well.

In welcoming and naming a child with this ceremony, we celebrate one of life's awe-inspiring moments, the birth of a human being and the continuation of humankind. We rejoice that this child has been born into the concern and care not only of his parents, but also of this gathering and community.

Memory Box & Importance of Wider Family

Olli now at 12 months is already familiar with the name we shall formally give him today. Above all else, a naming ceremony is about the expression of joy, the joy of Olli's life. It is also a time to consider our responsibilities towards him and all the children among us. By formally naming Olli we mark his individuality and uniqueness as a person. He already has displayed a unique trait that may get him entered into the Guinness World Book of Records for the fastest speed at crawling.

The phrase "it takes a village to raise a child" is true. And you are here today representing the larger community in which this child will grow up, and be known by his name.

Olli's parents will begin today a new family tradition. Jourdan has created for his son a memory box. Michelle & Jourdan in the coming months and years will place in the box mementos of Olli's childhood. When he is older at a time of their choosing they will have Olli open this treasured box of keepsakes and share its contents with him. Among its contents Olli's parents want him to find notes from all of you offering words of wisdom or thoughts that you feel would aid him on his journey through life. There is colored note paper set aside for you to write on after today's ceremony and we ask you to place your notes to Olli in the memory box before you leave to go home.

Promises from Family and Friends

All of you gathered here today, I will ask you all a question and we hope and trust that you will signify your commitment with one hearty affirmative response of "we will." Will you all give this child a heart-warming welcome -- and will you accept the privilege and the responsibility of helping to nurture Olli?

Assembly: We will

Celebrant: Being a grandparent, aunt or uncle is a joyful, tender and solemn duty, so will you family members agree to share your wisdom and will you respect, befriend and love Olli and be supportive of the decisions his parents make on his behalf? If so please say,

Assembly: We will

Appointment of Guideparents

Celebrant: Olli's Parents have chosen two very special individuals, Meghan & Fred, whom they hope will help shape their son's life. Children need role models who are not their parents. Michelle & Jourdan recognize that there will be times when they may not have the answers or Olli may not wish to discuss certain things with his parents. Their hope is that their son will be able to turn to Meghan or Fred for additional guidance and support. Meghan's husband Adam and Fred's wife

Jackie will play an important part as they support their spouses in their role as guideparents. They will also share a loving bond with Olli and be supportive of Olli's parents.

A guideparent is a mentor and a wise, trusted guide, an advisor who has nurtured a special relationship with a protégé that allows for the free exchange of ideas and advice. A mentoring relationship is meaningful and deeply rewarding to both child and mentor.

Meghan & Fred will you look upon this child with affection and will you give to him your guidance, friendship and inspiration?

Meghan and Fred: We will

Celebrant: Will you both as guideparents be supportive of Michelle and Jourdan and assist them with their duties as parents when needed?

Meghan and Fred: We will

Reading or poem

Guide Parent, Meghan will now read for us a poem
[Meghan reads]

Parental promises to the child and each other

Being a parent is an awesome responsibility. It is easy to focus so much time and attention on your child that you forget to carve out time for each other. You are an example to Olli of what a marriage should be. So, Michelle & Jourdan, in front of your family and friends do you both promise that you will continue to treasure the time you spend together as a couple, and support each other through the changes in your lives?

Michelle and Jourdan: We do

Celebrant: This wee one is so dear to you both. He has come into your lives and forever changed them, and now your role as parents has been embraced with responsibility, care and love, but not without fun as well.

Will you as parents, here before your friends and family, declare that you are committed to offer unconditional love to Olli and help him to find joy in living?

Michelle and Jourdan: We do

Celebrant: Do you both promise to protect and provide for Olli so he may grow up to be happy and safe? Do you vow to encourage his curiosity, courage and enthusiasm so that he can face life's challenges with resilience and optimism? Furthermore, do you promise to guide, respect, and support the choices he makes throughout his life? Do you commit to do your best to raise Olli to take his place in the community as a kind and caring individual?

Michelle and Jourdan: We do

Reading or poem

Celebrant: Guide Parent, Fred will now read a poem:

[Fred reads poem]

The Child's Entrance into the World

More than 80 percent of life on earth exists in its rivers, streams, lakes, and oceans. The poet Novalis said, "Our bodies are molded rivers." Indeed, a high percentage of the human body is made of water. The New York Times journalist and naturalist Hal Borland said, "From the time we stand in youthful wonder beside a spring or brook, till we sit in old age and watch the endless roll of the sea, we feel a strong kinship with the waters of this world."

It was only natural that Olli was born sliding through the waters of his birthing pool and rose out wet and glistening not unlike baby dolphins in the sea.

Olli entered the world in the early morning of October 10th in Hobart, Indiana at St. Mary's Hospital to the joy of his parents, family and friends.

Reason for the Child's Name

Olli's middle name, Brick, was chosen by both parents for a more personal reason. This was the name used by Jourdan's brother, Richard Michael, who sadly lost his life. He would really have loved Olli, and would have been a caring & dedicated uncle as well as a valuable source of advice.

The Naming

We give the child a name in this ceremony, and by doing so we declare that the child is an individual, a unique and a separate person with a dignity and a life of his own. A name once given will be associated forever with a face, a voice, a walk, a laugh and all of that comprises that person's unique attributes and individuality.

This child's name will be spoken, whispered, shouted, cried, sung and written – thousands of times, casually and meaningfully – by family, friends, neighbors, teachers, doctors, colleagues, strangers, and possibly someday by [his/her] own children and grandchildren. It will define [his/her] identity.

I now ask Olli's Parents and guideparents to gather in a semicircle around the child and each place a gentle hand on Olli. [Celebrant gently places hand on top of child's head & says]:

We this day dedicate and name this child and so henceforth may he be known as Olli (middle and last name).

A Blessing for Olli

May you find beauty in the wonders of this earth.
May you seek and find the internal beauty in others.
May happiness uplift you and may you share joy with others.
May your heart be peaceful and love surround you.
May you remember to lend a strong arm to others in need.

Olli Brick Smith's baby naming ceremony.

May you find courage so that fear does not rob you of your full potential.

May you seek truth even when others try to deceive you and keep your own words true.

May you seek reason and knowledge.

May joy and laughter fill your years.

May your name always bring honor to yourself and to your family.

Guideparents Lighting of the Candle

As all of you here have already discovered, Olli can light up a room with his presence. He will also need you all to be a light for him in the years to come. Having made their vows to Olli earlier, I now ask guideparents, Meghan and Fred, to come and light this candle as a symbol of their ongoing commitment to guide and light a path for Olli as he journeys through life. This support from his guideparents and all of you in turn will allow Olli to shine his own light out into the world.

In a little while I will present a certificate of Naming and ask the parents, guideparents & grandparents to join me to sign the Certificate.

Congratulations to you all!

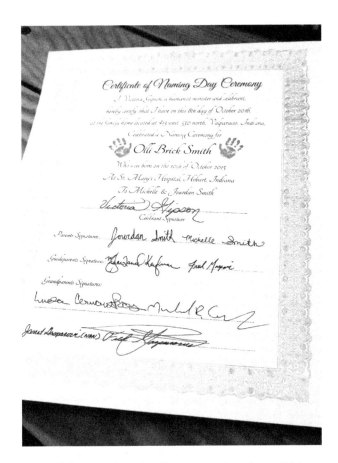

Celebrant Victoria Gipson made a beautiful certificate to commemorate Olli Brick Smith's baby naming ceremony.

Trans Naming Ceremonies

A trans naming ceremony is not that different from a baby naming ceremony in that a person is being introduced to their community and that giving their name is a special way of acknowledging their place in their world and their value to our communities. Both performing and attending a trans naming ceremony signals your acceptance and love for the person being named and can be an important part of affirming their worth.

In terms of structure, the ceremony is similar to a baby naming except that a trans naming ceremony won't have guideparents. You will consult with the individual looking to be named to find out exactly what they're looking for, who they'd like to include, and, as always, their preferred pronouns. Don't assume that a transwoman prefers she/her. Many trans people also embrace gender neutral terms such as they/them or xie.

Trans Naming Ceremony by Kenna Covington

Celebrant: Hi, everyone! Thank you everyone for joining us. It's a special day that we are sharing because we are celebrating one of the most shining lights among us in a ceremony that not only acknowledg-

Photo will be included in May, 2018 edition

es change, but self-determination, acceptance (both self and community driven), and above all, love.

I'd like to begin by taking a few deep breaths together. We breathe
in love and we breathe out peace. We breathe in hope and we breathe
out joy.

Thank you.

Today we recognize a new name and celebrate a life of integrity for the person many of us have known for years as Magdalene. We honor the name given to you by your parents. Every parent is given the opportunity to choose a name for their child, which any parent will tell you is a daunting task. Who will this little baby be? Babies grow and become toddlers, who gain nicknames like Maggie Moo or Moomoo.

Toddlers soon develop and grow into children who begin to claim their own identities. This name was chosen with love and potential for a life they couldn't see for you, but have always been ready and continue to help you claim. It's the unique combination of the name you've carried for thirteen years, your life, experiences, your hopes and fears, and also your dreams and aspirations that have brought you to this moment. We honor this name and release it to your history - and acknowledge that the time has come to declare a new name.

Today we are creating the sacred space that allows Troye to live his new identity fully in our community.

Troye, will you please come forward?

[Troye steps forward]

Troye, we know this has been a long journey for you. You have struggled to claim your right to live outwardly as you feel your true identity to be, a young man. Every human struggle to find their identity and place in the world, and yours has had more fear than most – real fear of what others may say or do, and by how our current culture denies the humanity of transgender people. Today, we are here, at a turning point – for all of us. It is an honor to be with you today, and to ask you: What is your new name?

Troye: My name is Troye.

Celebrant: This name now symbolizes all that you truly are and are becoming. I see you and I recognize you as Troye.

This is a turning point for all of us, because we have known and loved Maggie for thirteen years. Now we have the opportunity to know and love Troye. Loving is easy, and understanding comes with time and communication. This is an opportunity to love, to put our beliefs and values into action as we welcome every bit of who Troye is to this community. And so, beloved friends, I ask you:

Will you do all that you can to welcome Troye into the world? Will you love and support him and each other in becoming all that we have the potential to be?

Gathered: We will.

Celebrant: This name is the culmination of a journey of discovery, and at the same time, it is also a beginning. Young man before us, strong and full of life, you are on the cusp of adulthood and we stand with you. This community that has always stood by you moves forward with you as you find your place in the world.

Collectively, our deepest objective is that you feel this love and know that we celebrate the strength and conviction you have shown - to tell and show the world what you are made of. And that does not begin and end with gender.

It's your compassion, your drive, your curiosity, and kindness. It's your ability to question and think independently and critically.

It's your smile and your laugh, your sense of humor, and your moral compass.

What makes you, you, can't be measured on any chart or filled out on any form. The whole of who you are is what and who we celebrate today.

As if it was even ours to give, Troye, we welcome you to the world and invite you to find pleasure in all that it has to offer.

Family and friends, please join me as we lift our voices and cheers for Troye, who we celebrate today!

Vow Renewals

A vow renewal ceremony is a touching way to celebrate an important anniversary or to begin healing from a tough period in a marriage. Because of the variety of reasons couples have for choosing to renew their vows, there is no set "feel" to the ceremony. It may be a raucous party for a couple's fiftieth wedding anniversary or it may be a private and solemn ceremony with only you and the couple present. It can involve a wedding-like setting with the couple in formal wear, or it can be informal and quick. When consulting with the couple, as always, make sure that you understand their reasons for renewing their vows. You don't have to pry. A simple question such as, "What is it that makes it important for you to renew your vows at this point in time?" is sufficient. The couple may choose to tell you a lot or a little. Just take what they give you to help them craft a ceremony that meets their needs.

Some couples may prefer to have something that looks like a wedding service. In that case, you can write the vow renewal with many of the same elements you use in writing wedding services. The only differences will come in your opening words and in the vows themselves. Below are some sample vows for a vow renewal service.

Vows for a Renewal Service by Autumn Reinhardt-Simpson

To heal broken vows

(These vows are written so that both spouses can say them to each other, both accepting the ways in which they may have neglected to nurture their relationship and pledging to work together to repair it.)

Spouses: We stood together _____ years ago as, happy and carefree, we pledged ourselves to each other. We couldn't have known then just how difficult marriage can be and how, from time to time, we would let each other down. I, (name) stand here before you (name), to declare

A couple dances to celebrate their vow renewal ceremony.

to you that you are still the choice of my heart and that I promise to always try to be a better (husband, wife, spouse). Knowing now how hard lifelong partnership can be, I pledge to you my ongoing effort to repair and nurture the bond that we share.

223

To Celebrate an Important Anniversary

Spouses: It has been _____ years since we came before witnesses to pledge ourselves to each other. Since then, we have weathered all the various circumstances of life. We've seen the birth of our children as well as the death of friends. We bought our first house together and we also argued about who was going to do which chores. We saw our children off to university as we began to navigate retirement for ourselves. So many changes, and yet, here we are, still in love and ready to make the same pledge today that we made _____ years ago.

I (name), continue to take you, (name), to be the chosen partner of my lifetime. I vow to continue to love you just as much as I did _____ years ago. I vow to care for you as we continue to grow into our old age. I choose you today with all the love and respect that I felt for you _____ years ago.

Divorce Ceremonies

Some people might find the idea of a divorce ceremony strange. After all, why are we celebrating the dissolution of a partnership? However, divorce, like marriage, like death, is a profound life change and marking the occasion can be helpful in allowing someone to acknowledge their pain and move on. Divorce ceremonies can include the couple or it can be done for an individual person who needs their community's presence to help them heal.

Divorce Ceremony for One Person by Autumn Reinhardt-Simpson

Celebrant: There are moments in our lives in which we feel a keen need for the love and support of our community, our family, and our friends. In times of death and tragedy, our community rallies around us, holding us up when we can't stand on our own. This has always been the way humanity works. And yet, until recently, one of the most profound changes a person can undergo, the dissolution of a partnership, was considered a private matter. We, thinking we were respecting the privacy and feelings of the affected people, turned our faces away and talked as little as possible about the breakup of a marriage. In some cases, we participated in the shaming of people who recognized that their partnerships were no longer working, seeing it as a failure of character and perseverance.

We gather today to bury that narrative. Deep in our hearts, we know better. All of us have, at one time or another, experienced a breakup. We know the pain of loss of companionship. We are intimately aware of that feeling of inadequacy that often follows on its heels. Some of us can even remember that feeling of shame when we had to tell others about our new situation.

The truth is that relationships, like people, are dynamic. Failure to stay coupled until death is no failure but rather a testament to our ability to grow and change as human beings. We should no more feel guilty and shameful that we didn't stay married than a caterpillar should feel bad about becoming a butterfly. Change is the only constant in our world and that truth applies to relationships as much as to the natural world.

And yet, even with this knowledge embraced, the pain and feeling of isolation can persist. And that is why we are gathered today around our sister _____. As a community that loves and cares for her, we reject the idea that _____ must suffer alone, that she feel in any way less than who she is simply because a relationship has reached its natural end. So please, as a show of support and love, let's gather in a circle with _____ at the center.

[Everyone gathers]

Celebrant: Losing a beloved relationship can sometimes make us feel less worthy, as though our inability to resuscitate the relationship against all odds stains our character and makes us less than. For this reason, I'd like to invite _____'s friends and family to share with _____ some affirming words that will remind her of her worth as an individual and her special place in our hearts.

[Participants each share memories, read a poem, share a quote, or offer up any words to remind _____ of her impact on them.]

Celebrant: _____, now that you've heard from others how much they love and support you, and now that you understand the impact you've had on the lives of your family and friends, I'd like to ask you to take new vows. These vows are not made to another but to yourself alone, in the presence of this community. At the end of these vows, I will ask the community also to vow to uphold you in care and love.

_____, do you promise to name your feelings without judgment? To allow yourself to grieve without blaming yourself?

Participant: I do.

Celebrant: Do you promise to always have compassion on yourself as you move through the grief process and begin your new life?

Participant: I do.

Celebrant: Do you promise to lean on your community, your friends and family who love you, without reproaching yourself for weakness?

Participant: I do.

Celebrant: And to those gathered in love around _____, do you promise to support _____ and not be afraid of her grief?

All: We do.

Celebrant: And do you promise to encourage, support, and promote _____ in looking compassionately on herself?

All: We do.

Celebrant: And do you promise not to turn away from grief but instead to be ready to face, with _____, the complicated feelings and emotions of divorce?

All: We do.

[You may insert a naming ceremony here if the participant wishes to take back a former name or adopt a new one]

Celebrant: _____, you stand before a community of love which has come together today expressly to help you heal. Such community is an incredible gift. Please always remember your vows to each other and lean on each other when you feel you cannot stand alone.

I would like to end with a blessing.

May you, _____, go forth today in the loving arms of your family and friends to confront together the trials of the world. May today signal the beginning of a new and hopeful way of being both individually and together.

Adoption Ceremonies

Each year, thousands of children are adopted in the United States. An adoption ceremony can be a great way not only to introduce a new child to friends and family, but also to put a period on the end of what can be a very lengthy and emotional process for all. Adoption ceremonies can be performed privately for families or they can be bigger affairs involving the larger community.

Some important points to remember when consulting about adoption ceremonies are names and the role of birth parents. Names are important because some children, especially those born overseas, take on new names, or they may or may not have the same last name as one or both parents. If the child is keeping a birth name they received overseas, make certain that you are able to pronounce it correctly. This will help a child feel important and understood.

Birth families are a very sensitive issue. In some cases, children are adopted as part of an open adoption, meaning that the birth parents still play a role in the child's life and the adopted family may wish to have them present for the ceremony. On the other hand, adoptive parents of children adopted in difficult circumstances or who have been abandoned by birth parents may wish to have no mention made at all of the birth parents or the adoption story. As always, make sure you talk through every aspect with your clients to ensure the event is not traumatizing.

Photo will be included in May, 2018 edition

Adoption Ceremony by Autumn Reinhardt-Simpson

Celebrant: Welcome, everyone, on this joyous day! We've all been waiting so long for (child's full name) arrival and here we are.

Adoption is an amazing journey, filled with hope, anxiety, love, and anticipation. It's a veritable roller coaster of emotions! How will I know when I've found my child? Will my child love me? Will my new parents love me? In so many ways, the adoption process mirrors the process of preparing for birth. As parents, we worry about whether we can provide everything a child needs. We spend weeks preparing a new bedroom, preparing other siblings for the new arrival. And that moment when you finally hold your child …

And yet adoption is different in many ways, too. Instead of waiting nine months, parents sometimes wait years for their child. The waiting can be so hard, so frustrating. You just want your child! Sometimes parents must travel the entire length of the globe to find them and bring them home.

But in the end, parents are parents. We share a common hope and anxiety for our children, those born of our bodies and those born of others who we have chosen to adopt as our own. In this, there is no difference.

It is so beautiful to see so many people gathered today to welcome this child to their new home. Your presence signifies your love and support for this new family and (mother) and (father) are so happy to share their joy with you.

At this time, I'd like to invite (father) to share with us their adoption story.

[Father shares the adoption story]

Celebrant: Thank you. What a journey. And now I invite (mother) to place upon this table some mementos from (child's) early days. These items have significance in (child's) birth culture which she'd like to share with you.

[Mother shares items and stories from child's first days]
[Celebrant can insert here a poem, quote, or musical interlude]

Celebrant: (Mother and Father), I now invite you to recite together the promises you have made to (child).

[Parents recite promises]

[Celebrant can insert here a guideparents presentation and promises, if applicable]

Celebrant: And now, the moment we've all been waiting for! I present to you, the _____ family! (Mother and Father) are so thankful for your presence here today. May we all go forward with hope for the new life among us!

Humanist Invocations

An invocation is a statement meant to open an occasion such as a meeting, conference or gathering that is meant to give an official start to proceedings. In the past, an invocation was almost always intended as a way to "invoke" God's blessing for an event. However, invocations are a great way for humanists to dignify an occasion by asking those present to be mindful of the deeper meaning of the gathering and their role in it.

Invocations should be appropriate to the occasion and not contain any elements of complaint or "preaching." They are ideally meant to set the tone of the following event. Invocations should be brief and can be

Humanist celebrant Jocelyn Williamson delivers a secular invocation at the City of Longwood, Florida Commission Meeting.

anything from a quote to words you have written yourself to suit the moment. In the case of the latter, it is good to find out as much as you can about the institution and event at which you'll be speaking. As with any ceremony you perform, you want your words to be both relevant and to enhance the occasion. You can find more examples of humanist invocations by going to the Humanist Society's website and clicking on the "Invocations" tab.

Invocation Examples

Dr. Tiffany Green, a humanist celebrant in Richmond, Virginia was asked to give an invocation on a very important occasion, the Norfolk State University Founders' Day Breakfast. Her presence there was no accident. The breakfast had originally been billed as a Prayer Breakfast and the theme was "Forging Onward Through Prayer, Education, and Service." The Freedom from Religion Foundation intervened and, to the university's credit, they changed both the name and the theme of the event. Then they invited Tiffany to give the secular invocation alongside other speakers such as the Reverend Al Sharpton.[10]

Tiffany: "September 18, 1935, eighty-five scared and excited students began their first day of classes at the Norfolk Unit of Virginia Union University. It was during the Great Depression but we can be sure that they had great hopes and dreams for themselves and their children.

We stand here today in a time of great promise but also great peril. Advances in technology and science have opened doors that our foremothers and forefathers never could have imagined. Yet, structural barriers, such as poverty, racism, sexism and homophobia prevent our children from seizing all that the world has to offer. Battles that we thought had been won, such as the right to vote, the right to be educated and the right to breathe are being waged anew."

"Today I call upon all of us, nonbelievers, Christians, Muslims, Pagans, Hindus, Buddhists and more to draw upon the strength of our common humanity. To dig deep into the reservoirs of resilience that allowed us to survive and even thrive as a people since we arrived on the shores of Jamestown."

"To embrace the tradition of secular humanism is to recognize that like Dorothy from the Wizard of Oz, all that we need for greatness lies within. We can solve the great problems of this age and make the world a better place for all simply by working together. In the words of the great Marcus Garvey, "Up you mighty people! Accomplish what you will!"

"And thus today—the eightieth anniversary of the founding of what would become the great Norfolk

State University—our challenge is to convert justice for all from a pipe dream to a reality that we create every day. Our children deserve no less."

> Notice that Tiffany's speech meets all the requirements of a good invocation - it's short, it unites, rather than divides, and it recognizes and dignifies the occasion.

Herb Silverman, author and founder of the Secular Coalition for America

"In 2003, I was invited by a Charleston City Council member to give the invocation before a meeting. Nobody who heard my invocation was offended by it. However, when Mayor Joseph P. Riley introduced me, half the council members walked out because they knew I was an atheist and didn't return until it was time for the Pledge of Allegiance. As the protesting council members recited the Pledge, they turned toward me and bellowed the words 'under God.' Several days later, six favorable letters, some from Christians, appeared in the Charleston Post and Courier. It was extraordinary to see Christians side with atheists in South Carolina, against other Christians. One letter said: "It is most regrettable that during a time when the fight is so fierce to have all citizens' rights protected and respected, some of us would neglect to do the same for others. When any elected official demonstrates such lack of tolerance, especially while performing his official duties, those of us of conscience must speak out and voice our outrage."

Herb: Thank you for this opportunity to invoke a minority point of view. Each of us is a minority in some way. It might be race, religion, sexual orientation, nationality, or any other aspect in which we may be regarded as different. Each of us is also part of some majority. It is when we wear our majority hats that we need to be most mindful of how we treat others. We must pledge our best efforts to help one another, and to defend the rights of all our citizens and residents.

What divides us is not so much our religious differences in this diverse country, but the degree of commitment we have to equal freedom of conscience for all people. We are gathered today, both religious and secular members of our community, with the shared belief that we must treat our fellow human beings with respect and dignity.

In this invocation, I don't ask you to close your eyes, but to keep your eyes constantly open to the serious problems that city government can solve or improve. I don't ask you to bow your heads, but to look up at what you can accomplish by applying your considerable talents and experience to the issues that confront us.

As you work together on behalf of all who live in this city, may you draw strength and sustenance from one another through reason and compassion. I'd like to close in a bipartisan manner by quoting from two presidents I greatly admire — one a Republican and the other a Democrat.

First, the Republican: "When I do good, I feel good; when I do bad, I feel bad. That is my religion." Abraham Lincoln.

And now, the Democrat: "It's remarkable how much you can accomplish if you don't care who gets the credit." Harry S. Truman.

Herb's invocation is another example of a call to unity. Note that he doesn't even mention humanism! Herb's goal is to impress on the politicians gathered that their duty is not to humanism, atheism, religion, or anything other than to their constituency.

Humanist Blessings

A humanist blessing is about showing appreciation and gratitude, support and love. Rather than asking for a supernatural being to confer favor upon an individual or group of individuals, a humanist blessing asks for the blessing (good wishes) of those gathered. Blessings are great when gathering together in a humanist community and to mark special occasions. Blessings should be short and clearly evoke the feelings and sentiments of the event.

A Small Collection of Humanist Blessings by Autumn Reinhardt-Simpson

"May all of us gathered here leave today with a sense of peace. May we go forward renewed in our intention to fight injustice in our own community and around the world."

"As we gather together, as friends, as fellow workers in the cause of justice, let us remember our friends and fellow workers who have gone before us, blazing the trail that leads us to a better existence."

"Before we eat, let's give thanks to the farmers and workers who have made this food possible, as well as the hands that have prepared it. We are literally being nourished every day by the hard, often unrecognized, work of others."

"On the occasion of Jordan's graduation, let's send him forth with support and good thoughts as he begins his journey into the adult world."

"Let's take our strength in this time of tragedy from the support that has welled up among friends, turning bleak circumstances into hope."

You will most likely be called on to do weddings more than anything else. But there are also people who do parting ceremonies, ceremonies for coming of age, you name it! I was even asked to do a set of formal readings for an audience during my local group's Darwin Day events. And for Earth Day, I once held a ceremony in which we likened our tree planting to the general rebirth experienced during springtime. An acquaintance of mine, also a celebrant, held a menarche party for his niece. Humanist celebrant Victoria Gipson does what she calls "Wise Woman" ceremonies to honor women's life transitions. So, give rein to your creative impulses and don't assume that you need to stick to the traditional ceremonies everyone is used to or even the ones mentioned in this chapter. Life is full of moments just waiting to be celebrated or marked in a special way.

CHAPTER 6

The Business of Love and Death

Part of being a celebrant is knowing how to run a small business. Some of you may already have this experience but for those who don't, it can be a little overwhelming. You'll need to know the laws in your area about small businesses and taxation as well as how to advertise and keep records. I hope this section gives you some tools to get started, but to maximize your learning, you may want to visit your community's Small Business Development Center. These centers exist to support small business growth in the community and they offer everything from seminars to one-on-one help. Until then, you're stuck with me so let's get started.

First Steps

There are a few things to keep in mind when running a small business. First of all, you will want to craft a business plan. You don't need anything exceptional but you will benefit significantly if you at least have a sense of where you want your business to go. You can find free online business plan templates at www.bplans.com. After you create a business plan, you can then create one, five, and ten-year goal plans. Keep in mind that your goals may change as you gain experience but having something to work toward is a great way to stay motivated and ensure that your business doesn't get stale and out of touch. Some questions you may want to consider when writing your plan are:

- Which services do I want to provide? For instance, will I do funerals/ memorials or just weddings? Baby namings? Trans naming ceremonies? Am I comfortable with divorce ceremonies?
- Who is my target demographic?
- How much will I charge?

Those are just a few of the questions you'll want to think about as you envision your business. You can then take this plan and use it to come up with your one, five, and ten-year goal plans and you'll soon be adulting your way into the small business world.

Secondly, you need a name! What will you call your business? Look back at your business plan as you think about this and consider your target demographic. You will want the name to reflect what it is you do as well as set the tone you want for your business. Check around to see what names other celebrants are using and, most importantly, see what domain names are already taken online! Nothing is worse than coming up with a great name and URL only to find that the domain name has been taken.

Once you've settled on a name, you'll need to open a business bank account and get set up to receive online payments. Though neither of these is a necessity, it will make your life easier. Having a separate bank account from your personal one will make keeping track of finances and taxes so much simpler. And being set up for taking payments online means fewer trips to the bank. More on that later.

And finally, you will most certainly want to do market research. This means checking out what other celebrants and officiants in your area charge for services, which services they perform, what their online ratings are like, etc. Get to know what it is they offer and review their websites so that you can be prepared to offer something different.

Let's talk now about other aspects of running a small business such as communication, contracts, collaborative tools, record keeping, advertising, organization, and your legal obligations.

Client Communication

Communication is probably the single most important thing for your small business. You'll need to be clear in your communication with clients to ensure that you understand their needs and that they understand what is expected of them as well. This is especially important when crafting your contract. You need to be as clear as possible about what everyone's roles are and how much you are charging for each aspect of your services. You should never perform any ceremony without having a signed contract. This will protect both you and your clients as it clearly spells out the responsibilities of both parties. Your contract does not have to be many pages long. All you need to do is cover the necessities. For example, check out the contract I used when I was a celebrant in Richmond, Virginia. It is adapted from the example given to new celebrants by the Humanist Society.

Secular Ceremonies RVA

Wedding/Commitment Ceremony Contract

Best wishes for your celebration and your life together!

Nonreligious couples, humanists, freethinkers and the interreligious frequently come to a humanist celebrant to help them celebrate a marriage. While I make no doctrinal or philosophical demands of any couple, I do have some basic requirements for couples who wish me to officiate at their ceremony. If, after reading over my policies and guidelines you wish to contract with me as your officiant, please return the Wedding/Commitment Ceremony Reservation Form with your check for $50, payable to Autumn Reinhardt-Simpson.

These are the requirements of the contract:

1. The basic cost for my officiating at a wedding/commitment ceremony is $300.00, $50 of which is the non-refundable deposit you will return with the Reservation Form. The remaining balance of $250.00 is due two weeks BEFORE your ceremony unless you have made alternative arrangements with me. Should you decide to

cancel the ceremony after paying the full amount, but more than 24 hours before the ceremony, I will refund all but the $50 deposit.

2. You are responsible for obtaining the space where the ceremony will be held, as well as (per state law) obtaining a valid Marriage License from the County Clerk's office. I will ensure that said license is properly filed with the Clerk's office following the ceremony.

3. I will be the Celebrant performing the ceremony. If you wish another clergy member to co-officiate with me, please give me their contact information. Please understand however, that by signing this contract you are choosing me to be your main Officiant, and that the ceremony will be as you and I have agreed to, and not the invited clergy.

4. You and I must meet either in person or online to plan your ceremony. There is no "set" Humanist wedding/commitment ceremony service. It is important that all the words spoken at your service be appropriate to you and for that reason I will provide you with example services, readings, vows, etc. from which you may choose or you may choose to write your own instead. You are welcome and encouraged to invite family and friends to participate in your ceremony.

5. Please remember that while I'm happy to offer the community a nontheistic alternative for ceremonies, this is a civil service and not an obligation. If at any time I decide that your ceremony should not go forward, I have the right to return your deposit and any payments made and cancel your service.

If you have any questions, please feel free to contact me either by phone (insert number) or email (insert email).

By signing this contract, I agree to the aforementioned requirements,

Signed _____

Printed Signature _____

Date _____

Signed _____

Printed Signature _____

Date _____

Officiant Signature _____

Printed Signature _____

Date _____

As you can see, it is very simple, easy to read, and gets the job done. Once a couple signs the contract and sends it to me. I sign it, scan, and return a signed copy to them.

The other form I like to give my clients is the reservation form. This form ensures that I have the dates and places of the ceremony and rehearsal all in one spot. You may wish to combine your contract and reservation forms - whatever works for you! Here is my reservation form: adapted from the example given to new celebrants by the Humanist Society.

Secular Ceremonies RVA

Wedding/Commitment Ceremony Reservation Form

Please fill out and return this form, along with your $50 deposit payable to Autumn Reinhardt-Simpson, to:

Autumn Reinhardt-Simpson, Humanist Celebrant

(Address)

Full Legal Names and Contact Information of Participants

Name: _____

Address: _____

_____

_____

Phone: _____

Email: _____

Name: _____

Address: _____

_____

_____

Phone: _____

Email: _____

Date and Time of Ceremony _____

Address of Venue _____

Date and Time of Rehearsal _____

Address of Venue _____

We have read the contract for Weddings/Commitment Ceremonies. A check for $50 is attached; we understand that if we choose not to use the services of Autumn Reinhardt-Simpson as humanist celebrant, this $50 is non-refundable. We also understand that the celebrant reserves the right at any time to decline or cancel this ceremony, in which case the deposit as well as any fees paid will be returned to us in full. We agree to pay the remaining $250 at least two weeks prior to our ceremony unless we make other arrangements with the celebrant.

Signature _____

Date _____

Signature _____

Date _____

Tools for Communication

A big part of good communication is the tools you use. While a face-to-face meeting is always nice, there will be times when a client wants to talk to you but is unable to meet in person. This is where Skype and Google Hangouts can become useful tools. I once had to plan a wedding for a couple that was living thousands of miles away and Hangouts became our primary mode of communication. It allowed us to actually see and hear each other and to gather more information from the interaction than had we just been on the phone or writing emails. If you're new to online video communication, don't worry! Both Skype and Hangouts are very easy to learn and work with. Just watch a few video tutorials on YouTube and you'll quickly get the hang of either one. Bonus - both are free. Check out https://hangouts.google.com and www.skype.com to get started.

Collaborating with Clients

Some celebrants are still using the postal service to mail out contracts and receive payment, and some celebrants are collaborating with clients on ceremonies via email - sending suggestions, changes, and new drafts back and forth. However, there are more efficient ways of getting all these tasks done.

For writing a ceremony with my clients, I like to use Google Docs because it allows myself and the client to edit a ceremony simultaneously while being in different locations. Google Docs is visually similar to Microsoft Word but with some added features. You and your clients can edit and make suggestions on the same document at the same time without having to make multiple drafts or deal with awkward editing features. It is also easy to share sample ceremonies and send contracts and invoices through your Drive (see below). The best parts about it are that it saves automatically, allows you to view past edits, make comments, have real-time conversations, and the Drive is cloud based, meaning you can access your documents from any machine, not just the one you used to make the original document. If you don't know how to use Google Docs or any of the Google Suite, there are literally thousands of tutorials online.

Microsoft Word now also features a cloud-based version that functions similarly but unlike Google, it has a price tag. Both are fantastic ways to share documents with your clients and make communication much easier. I strongly recommend that you become familiar with and use one of these two options. Not only are most clients expecting seamless editing and sharing these days but it will simply make your life much easier.

Recordkeeping

Keeping good records is vital to your business. If you're old fashioned and enjoy keeping paper records and you can do it well, by all means, keep doing it. There is no sense in changing your system if it truly works for you. However, many people find that technology does a much better job at keeping things both organized and easily retrievable. If you prefer technology, my suggestion is to use either Google Drive or Microsoft OneDrive. You already have Google Drive if you have a Gmail address. Google Drive is a cloud based storage system which makes all your documents retrievable via any device. This is where, for instance, your Google Docs are stored. My favorite way to use either of these drives is to create a folder for my business and, within that, separate folders for all my clients. I keep signed contracts (you can scan these in if they're paper-based and shred the originals to save space), copies of ceremonies and anything else related to my work with them in the separate client folders. It is easy to retrieve and, best of all, I can quickly and easily share individual documents in my Drive with clients. If you need help learning Google Drive, there are lots of tutorials out there. You can download Google Drive even if you are an Apple user.

Microsoft OneDrive is similar to Google Drive in most instances.

It is very important that you keep signed paperwork, either hard-copy or digital, for at least seven to ten years before destroying it. Make sure you are regularly cleaning and organizing whatever storage system you use so that it doesn't become cluttered and be sure to shred documents, rather than just recycling them whole.

Personal Organization

Aside from keeping good records, you need to be an organized and timely person yourself. That means keeping a calendar, either electronic or paper, and sticking with it. My own habit was to immediately enter the date of the ceremony and any rehearsals into my calendar upon receiving my deposit. I then calculated how much time I'd need to write and collaborate/revise the ceremony and put due dates into my calendar as well. Finally, I entered the dates for invoices to go out. With all these reminders in place, it was really easy to stay focused and on time.

Pro Tip

"Don't be surprised or anxious if a ceremony doesn't start at the specified time. None of the ones I've officiated have started on time, which means they also may run longer than anticipated. I recommend not scheduling consecutive ceremonies too close to each other. Assume an average 15 minute delay in the start time and buffer your arrival and departure accordingly. I've heard about officiants who are notoriously late because they don't schedule well for the distance and traffic. Don't be those guys. Schedule generously for yourself and your clients' peace of mind."

- Keith Robinson, humanist celebrant, Hampton Roads, VA

Legal Obligations

Every state and province is different but generally speaking, once you are endorsed as a humanist celebrant, you must then register as clergy with your state or province before performing any marriages. Just because you have an endorsement from the Humanist Society does not mean you are automatically legally able to perform a wedding in your state or province. Make sure you understand your local and state laws regarding those who can perform marriages before you sign any contracts with clients. The Humanist Society has a listing of marriage laws by state [http://thehumanistsociety.org/celebrants/resources/laws/] but you should always double check with your local city or county clerk's office to get the most up-to-date information. If you have any issues with the local clerk's office, you can contact the Appignani Humanist Legal Center at the American Humanist Association. Their lawyers are there specifically to help you with these kinds of issues if you're unfortunate enough to run into them.

Although I myself followed all the above suggestions regarding legality, this still turned out to be quite a scenario for me! After being endorsed by the Humanist Society, I had to register with the City of Richmond (Virginia) clerk. However, the clerk was suspicious of my endorsement and denied it, saying that I did not meet the necessary requirements. I had studied the applicable laws regarding who can marry people in the state of Virginia and I knew that I not only met the requirements but exceeded them. The problem was that there was an understanding by many county and city clerks (which was not part of the law) that officiants had to have a physical church building and congregation. Because I had studied the laws, I felt confident asking for a hearing with a judge to contest my rejection. The Appignani Humanist Legal Center was instrumental in helping me acquire affidavits and other necessary legal paperwork for my hearing. When I finally went to court, the judge agreed that humanist celebrants in Virginia were in compliance with the law. That said, all officiants must still register with their clerk and, at the time of this writing, some in Virginia are still having trouble with suspicious clerks. Be prepared to state your case and don't be afraid to ask for a hearing with a judge!

Another important legal issue is to make sure you are aware of your responsibilities regarding the signed marriage license. Most states require the officiant to return the signed license after the wedding ceremony. I always bring a stamped envelope with me to ceremonies so that I can sign, seal, and mail the license while leaving the venue. Most jurisdictions will impose penalties on any officiant who does not return a signed license within a specified amount of time.

Some couples have no idea how to go about getting married and they may ask you if you provide the license. Always refer your clients to the proper government website dealing with marriage licenses in your jurisdiction. It is always the clients' responsibility to obtain the license and usually yours to return it signed to the clerk. As stated earlier in the section specifically dealing with weddings, I find that it is a good idea to have the couple sign the marriage license just before the wedding ceremony begins to avoid having to fight for the couple's attention afterwards.

Determining Your Rates

Most celebrants advertise and charge for their services while some provide them free or for a donation. Whichever you choose is entirely up to you. That said, it can be hard to determine what you're worth. Take a look around you and scope out the market. What are other officiants in your area charging? Visit the websites of a few local marriage commissioners and other officiants and compare. Remember that you are crafting unique ceremonies, not providing boilerplate like some officiants, and should charge accordingly. Never forget traveling expenses! When I traveled outside my metro area, I assessed a per mile gas fee and also included any hotel charges which I clearly listed on my website. I didn't charge meal expenses but you might decide to do so. Some celebrants also add a charge for being present at rehearsals.

Another option is tiered pricing. For instance, I had three levels of pricing. For $300, I would write, edit, collaborate and officiate a personalized wedding ceremony for the couple. $150 was for the rare client who wanted to write the entire ceremony themselves with only moderate additions or revisions made by me, or for those who needed to get married quickly and wanted to use one of my pre-made quick scripts. For $50, I would come by and simply sign the marriage license. This was for couples who wanted absolutely no ceremony at all but just needed someone to ask the necessary legal questions and provide the signature.

When it comes to funerals and memorials, some celebrants charge while others do not. Remember that either way you do it, you're still putting in a lot of work, often at short notice, and it is perfectly okay to charge for that work. Another option is accepting a donation. Again, tiered pricing might be a good option here, charging one amount for at-need clients and another for pre-need clients.

After deciding what your base charge is you should determine a deposit for your clients. ALWAYS get a deposit from your clients before taking on any work. I usually request a deposit to come along with the contract and reservation form. That allows me to formally put the date on my calendar and begin work. No deposit, no work. My deposit is $50 non-refundable unless I myself cancel the ceremony. I specify in my contract that I should receive the remainder of the money no later than two weeks prior to the ceremony. Any ceremony that is to take place within two weeks of booking must be paid in full at the time of booking. There is a benefit to collecting your fee two weeks before the wedding rather than on the day. It means that checks (when used) can clear and that you don't have to awkwardly ask for it during the festivities.

Another way to handle payment (and one I highly suggest) is via PayPal, Google Wallet, or Apple Pay. This eliminates delay and the need for stamps and envelopes. You will likely have clients that prefer old fashioned check writing but the majority will find the ease and efficiency of one of the other services preferable.

Because you'll most likely be working with your clients over an extended period of time, the best practice is to send them an invoice a month before the date of their ceremony to remind them of what's still due. The internet is full of invoice templates that you can easily download and customize but you might also want to design your own, perhaps with your logo on it. Make sure you file the invoice with your other documents relating to your client, either in a folder on your computer or in a regular folder in a paper-based system. If using a paper-based system, it is worth buying a PAID stamp from an office supply store so that you can keep track of which invoices have been paid in full.

Provinces, states, and even cities have their own rules when it comes to running a small business. Make sure you are aware of which taxes need to be paid and if you need a business license to operate in your city. Generally speaking, you will only need a business license if you make over a certain amount of money each year as a celebrant. However, always check. When tax time comes (usually quarterly for businesses), you'll find it is much easier to weather if you've kept accurate and updated records. It's very easy to keep a spreadsheet of all your expenses and fees paid and even easier to transfer those numbers to your tax forms.

Advertising

But how to get clients in the first place? Your best first stop is your local humanist group. Make sure you attend meetings and have business cards printed to hand out among the group. Your business cards don't need to be fancy but they should clearly state what it is you do. It's not enough to have "humanist celebrant" and a website.

My business cards, made in the same colors and style as my website, list the types of ceremonies I offer on the back. Another idea is to give workshops in your community on writing ceremonies, perhaps even giving a workshop in writing memorials. Some funeral homes also keep a list of officiants and you should definitely get your name on them. Network and trade business cards with vendors you like working with

Example of Hamish Tear's business card, humanist celebrant from Wyoming.

and register yourself as an officiant willing to give an invocation at your city council meetings.

Another good idea is to think of places where you can regularly keep a stock of business cards or brochures such as your apartment building lobby or the bulletin board at your grocery store. Check in with these locations once a month to restock or freshen up worn out materials.

Finally, and most importantly, is online advertising. You may be new at this but you can do it! First of all, you need a website. Though there are do-it-yourself platforms like Wix and WordPress, I recommend spending a few extra bucks for a web designer. As the world's most challenged designer of web-based content, I strongly urge you to do this! You may be great with design but a web designer will have all kinds of great psychological tips and tricks to create a really arresting website for you that will pay back in no time. They might also help you design a logo which is a really great idea. This may all sound like window dressing but having good design will go far in conveying legitimacy for your business. It will also enhance the usability of your site, something clients will appreciate. I recommend having a section of your site that describes what a

*Celebrant Scott Rhoades has created several Pinterest boards to
give his couples endless wedding ideas.*

humanist celebrant is (include a link to the Humanist Society website)
and what your endorsement means. You can even include a copy of your
endorsement certificate. You can also include a page with your contracts
and reservation forms which will make it easy for potential clients to see
whether you might be a good fit ahead of time. Another great idea is to

have a page that tells clients how to obtain a marriage license. Your site should be as much of a one-stop shop as possible, including testimonials from past clients and photos of ceremonies you have officiated.

Emily Wren Photography

Websites are a great way to increase your visibility and show your level of professionalism.

Next up, make a Facebook or Instagram (or both!) account for your business and make sure you collect ratings from past clients. You may hate social media but it really is a great way to advertise almost effortlessly. Besides posting your own news regarding the business, you can post general interest articles on humanism, weddings, funerals and other ceremonies. Make sure to publish content often to keep your audience's eyes on your page, preferably at least once every two days. Don't forget to list your social media sites on your business cards and don't be shy about asking clients for a review.

Besides the usual website and social media pages, it's important to have your business listed on sites like Thumbtack, Wedding Wire, The Knot, and others that couples go to when first beginning their search for officiants and vendors. Some of these sites offer free listings in addition to their premium (paid) listings, so it is possible to get your name out there without a financial investment. During my time in Virginia, I estimate that 90 percent of my clients found me via Wedding Wire alone. These free sites are also a great place to list your client reviews! It's okay to suggest to a satisfied client that they leave a quick review on your listing.

Also consider attending bridal shows. Set up an attractive booth for yourself and don't forget to bring along your calendar just in case someone wants to book right away! Having a few goodies or giveaways on hand is always a good idea.

Beautiful photos on your Knot listing really help your page stand out!

Pro Tip

"Something I like to do in addition to making sure the family has my contact info and extra business cards, is to give the wedding couple a personal gift. I usually type up the ceremony in a nice font and layout, do a simple binding and present it to them after the ceremony. Sometimes I also buy a little gift that may have some meaning within their ceremony. I always put my contact and website on anything I give them."

–Joshua Lewis Berg, humanist celebrant,
Huntington Woods, Michigan

All these tips will go far in helping you advertise your services but nothing replaces just doing a great job. If you can craft, create, and facilitate memorable ceremonies as well as work well with your clients, you will soon establish a word-of-mouth reputation that no amount of advertising could generate.

CHAPTER 7

Applying for Endorsement

Not everyone who reads this book is looking to become endorsed by the Humanist Society. In fact, not everyone reading this book is even a humanist. However, if you are looking for endorsement by the Humanist Society,[11] this chapter will walk you through the necessary steps.

First and foremost, you'll need the application! You can find it on The Humanist Society website: http://thehumanistsociety.org/. There is a tab at the top that says "Apply" with a drop-down menu. When you click on Endorsements Available, it will take you to a list of all the endorsements given by the Society. What you choose will depend on your situation.

Associate Humanist Celebrant

This endorsement is a one-time endorsement that expires after ninety days. If the applicant wishes to continue after ninety days, they must apply for the regular celebrant status (see below). The associate humanist celebrant is a good pick for those who want to officiate just one wedding, or for those who need time to familiarize themselves with humanism. If you apply to become a humanist celebrant and show promise, but do not yet demonstrate a knowledge of humanism, the Humanist Society Board of Directors may recommend that you receive associate humanist celebrant endorsement instead. Don't be disappointed if this happens! It means that all you need to do in the next few months is become better acquainted with humanist philosophy and practice!

Humanist Celebrant

This is the endorsement most people seek when they are looking to become the equivalent of clergy and be legally able to marry clients after registering locally. The initial endorsement is valid for two years. After the initial two years, you have the opportunity for re-endorsement. If re-endorsed, your certificate is valid for five years. Humanist celebrants who have received this endorsement are not automatically able to perform legal wedding ceremonies. Each celebrant must still register with their county, state, or province and fulfill all proper legal requirements before they can be legally recognized as an officiant in their locality. Failure to understand this can impact your business negatively, not to mention the possibility that it can nullify any marriages you perform. Get registered!

Humanist Lay Leader (Military)

Because the United States military does not presently allow for humanist chaplains, the lay leader is someone who works to coordinate within the chaplaincy office to facilitate humanist gatherings. Though lay leaders are encouraged to eventually apply for full celebrant endorsement, some may opt to remain lay leaders. This endorsement is great for any military personnel who are looking to create a more organized humanist community on their base.

Humanist Chaplain

The humanist chaplain works or volunteers within secular institutions such as universities, prisons, nursing units, hospices, and hospitals. Their role is to represent humanism to humanists and non-humanists alike, much in the way a Christian chaplain works with Christians and non-Christians within an institutional setting. The Humanist Society will only give this endorsement to those working or volunteering within institutions and re-endorsement depends on the applicant having had sufficient work in an institutional setting during their initial endorsement period. In other words, you can't just apply to become a chaplain if you have no intention of working or volunteering with both humanists and non-humanists within an institution. This endorsement is a good option for humanists in divinity school or who work in social work settings. Remember, however, that many institutions that use the services of chaplains will often require that a chaplain have undergone CPE (clinical pastoral education), a process that can take many years and requires study as well as practicum.

Humanist Chaplain and Celebrant Dual Endorsement

This dual endorsement is meant for chaplains who also want to be able to legally perform weddings (being a chaplain does not confer this right).

Application Requirements

Now that you are familiar with the different endorsements offered by the Humanist Society, we'll concentrate on the application requirements for the most common endorsement - humanist celebrant.

The qualifications for the endorsement are:
- A completed online application
- Three references from non-relatives (this includes in-laws)
- $40 application fee
- $100 annual professional fee
- Member of the American Humanist Association
- Understanding of humanism and the humanist celebrant role

The application will require you to demonstrate that you understand humanism, especially as it is described in the Humanist Manifesto III. You can find a copy of this on the American Humanist Association website as well as in the appendices of this book and I recommend that you get cozy with it. As you read it, think about how it applies to your own life and philosophy. This will give you plenty to write about on your application. The application will also ask you what you believe to be the role of a celebrant. Of course, you've read this book so you should have a pretty good understanding of what that entails.

There is always that one dreaded question on any application and it always has to do with weaknesses. Many people think that this means that they should say that their one weakness is that they are just so darn hard-working! In our case, the question is phrased differently. "In what ways do you feel unqualified to fulfill the duties of a humanist celebrant?" You should answer very truthfully. The purpose of this question is not to identify and root out "bad people with bad answers" but rather to be able to allow you to identify areas with which you need more guidance. It might be that you could use more help in public speaking or perhaps you don't quite have enough resources to help you get started writing original ceremonies. Whatever your area of difficulty is, don't be afraid to mention it. This question is followed by one which asks if you would like help in identifying opportunities to improve. In my opinion, all of us could use continual education and improvement!

Finally, you'll need references from three people who know you well enough to comment on your ability to be a celebrant. This is very important. You don't want to ask your boyfriend or the person you met at the library last week to be your reference. Ideally, most references for any purpose should come from people to whom you are unrelated and who have known you at least two years. The best-case scenario would be references from people who have worked with you in humanist groups or on projects that required commitment, integrity, and good communication skills. Other clergy make excellent references, as do bosses, and supervisors. Try not to have a friend write your reference unless they can speak about you as a professional or a volunteer.

Once you've completed your application and paid the application fee, your next hurdle is the interview. Someone from the Humanist Society Board of Directors will arrange to speak with you about your application within a couple of weeks. Don't be nervous about this chat! It is very informal and is meant to allow the board to get to know who you are. It's also a great time for you to elaborate on the good points in your application as well as to bring up anything not mentioned. I've personally always had fun when chatting with members of the board and they have always been willing to give me ideas and resources.

The Humanist Society offers many different kinds of endorsements to suit the needs of a large humanist community worldwide. If you apply for one endorsement, don't be surprised if the Society tries to match you up with another. For instance, if you apply to become a celebrant, the Society may get in touch to recommend that you reapply to become an associate humanist celebrant instead. This is not because there is anything wrong with you! The Humanist Society is excited about your interest and wants to make sure that you get the proper education and training necessary for full celebrant endorsement. The suggestion that you be an associate humanist celebrant first is an acknowledgement that you have the potential to become a great humanist celebrant with just a little more training and experience. The Humanist Society is committed to working with you to make sure that you are fully prepared to take on any leadership roles in our larger humanist community. Take every opportunity that is given to you to grow your skills!

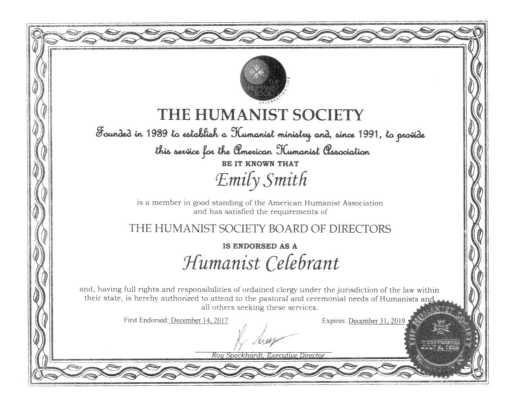

Above is the certificate all humanist celebrants receive once they are endorsed by the Humanist Society.

Afterword

In writing an afterword, an author often tries to leave the reader with encouraging and inspiring words with which to send them out into the world. My own intention was to write about the growth of secular ceremony and the need for the humanist community to embrace it, rather than run from it as a "religious" hangover. I wanted to encourage celebrants and other readers alike that, as humanists (or the nonreligious) we have just as much right to our own ceremonies as anyone else. But as I began to write my original afterword, I discovered that my good and far more poetic friend Anne Barker had written pretty much everything I wanted to say and that therefore, I should leave it to her. So, I have included here something that Anne originally wrote for a different part of the book but which puts a rather eloquent and inspiring period to the end of what has largely been my own rather instructional writing.

And so, I give you Anne's wise words as a parting gift:

"Every rite of passage holds different meanings for everyone involved and the possible combinations are endless. We may be celebrating a marriage – and simultaneously remembering our own wedding day … or the wedding that didn't happen … or the loss of a love, or a loved one. We might be evaluating the commitment of the people before us, or re-evaluating our own commitments. We may be considering how weddings, or marriage, have changed over time. We may be elated, jealous, sad and celebratory, all at once.

"At a funeral – we hear one version of a person's story. We reflect on what we know to be true of their life … reflect on our own accomplishments or losses … imagine our own funerals … relive our memories, our joys, and our grief.

"At a child dedication or naming ceremony – we ponder our responsibility to the child …think about our own children, or lack of children … possibly celebrate, grieve, regret and be moved, simultaneously.

"Each rite of passage is a doorway, an invitation. An opportunity exists – a ritual to engage with. It stirs, within us, our own feelings and commitments. Whether we are about to be married, watching from the back row, or officiating the service, a wedding calls us into a reflection on human re-lationships – all relationships – and invites us to engage. A memorial calls us to these relationships as well. A naming ceremony, a home blessing, a coming out celebration, all the same. Whether we accept the invitation or not, that is entirely personal. The ritual provides a doorway – a potent moment of transition. Each individual chooses whether to walk through … which path to follow … what meaning will be made.

"Never let anyone tell you that ceremony is unimportant or outdated. Rites of passage are touchstone moments in our lives, places where we pause, reflect, evaluate, and often reshape our own life experience and direction. A memorial provokes us to think: 'How can we help this family? how do I want to be remembered?' A home blessing encourages us to check in: '"Is my home a safe, celebratory, healthy place?' A union asks us 'How will we support these people in their goals? How are my relation-ships going?' Rituals to mark what were once deemed 'negative events' – like divorce – help people to mark a clear, definitive moment of transi-tion, and invite close community members to help with the passage.

"As officiant, your most essential task is to hold and nurture that space for people to enter into. That's all. They will go on their own journey, do their own work, in their own time. That is not up to you. You offer them the space – frame the doorway – and leave them to their task. It is a powerful honour, and a profound invitation for you, as well.

"Rites of passage are like a doorway."

Anne Barker

June 2, 2016

About the Author

Autumn Reinhardt-Simpson is an American author, celebrant, and feminist theologian now living in Canada. When not writing, she gets her kicks as a competitive powerlifter. You can view her ongoing writing projects on her website electriceelpond.com.

The Humanist Manifestos

A History of the Manifesto

The first Humanist Manifesto was written in 1933 and signed by thirty-four people then active in the movement. Many of the signatories were Unitarian Universalist ministers and nontheistic religious people who saw no contradiction between a nontheistic religious outlook and humanism. Indeed, the first incarnation of the manifesto saw humanism as a new religion without dogma and creeds, and it laid out in fifteen points its overall vision for a better society. It borrowed sentiments from the socialist movement popular at that time as it railed against societies more interested in profit than people, and urged voluntary cooperation in achieving lasting peace. It could be said that the first manifesto was less concerned with the particularities of individual nontheistic religious belief and more interested in uprooting a theology that had been used in the service of oppression.

In 1973, Paul Kurtz and Edwin Wilson wrote the Humanist Manifesto II. The authors looked back at the previous manifesto with eyes newly opened by the tragedies of World War Two. In their opinion, the first manifesto was too optimistic about the future even though Kurtz and Wilson continued to hope that war and poverty would someday end. Their new manifesto, like the first, reflected the debates of the time with the new version offering support for human rights and opposition to nuclear destruction. The second manifesto, however, departed somewhat in its acceptance of nontheistic religion and religious language and the authors put more emphasis on a nontheism outside of religious structures.

The most recent Humanist Manifesto (Humanist Manifesto III) cements the American Humanist Association's shift away from an emphasis on religious humanism and toward secular humanism. This latest incarnation of the manifesto, rather than laying out its objections to traditional religion, instead focuses on humanism's potential to transform the way we view our commitments to the earth and to each other.

Understanding the genesis and particularities of each manifesto is important for those wishing to become endorsed by the Humanist Society. Therefore, each manifesto is reproduced here by kind permission of the American Humanist Association.

The Humanist Manifesto (1933)

The time has come for widespread recognition of the radical changes in religious beliefs throughout the modern world. The time is past for mere revision of traditional attitudes. Science and economic change have disrupted the old beliefs. Religions the world over are under the necessity of coming to terms with new conditions created by a vastly increased knowledge and experience. In every field of human activity, the vital movement is now in the direction of a candid and explicit humanism. In order that religious humanism may be better understood we, the undersigned, desire to make certain affirmations which we believe the facts of our contemporary life demonstrate.

There is great danger of a final, and we believe fatal, identification of the word religion with doctrines and methods which have lost their significance and which are powerless to solve the problem of human living in the Twentieth Century. Religions have always been means for realizing the highest values of life. Their end has been accomplished through the interpretation of the total environing situation (theology or world view), the sense of values resulting therefrom (goal or ideal), and the technique (cult), established for realizing the satisfactory life. A change in any of these factors results in alteration of the outward forms of religion. This fact explains the changefulness of religions through the centuries. But through all changes religion itself remains constant in its quest for abiding values, an inseparable feature of human life.

Today man's larger understanding of the universe, his scientific achievements, and deeper appreciation of brotherhood, have created a situation which requires a new statement of the means and purposes of religion. Such a vital, fearless, and frank religion capable of furnishing adequate social goals and personal satisfactions may appear to many people as a complete break with the past. While this age does owe a vast debt to the traditional religions, it is none the less obvious that any religion that can hope to be a synthesizing and dynamic force for today must be shaped for the needs of this age. To establish such a religion is a major necessity of the present. It is a responsibility which rests upon this generation. We therefore affirm the following:

FIRST: Religious humanists regard the universe as self-existing and not created.

SECOND: Humanism believes that man is a part of nature and that he has emerged as a result of a continuous process.

THIRD: Holding an organic view of life, humanists find that the traditional dualism of mind and body must be rejected.

FOURTH: Humanism recognizes that man's religious culture and civilization, as clearly depicted by anthropology and history, are the product of a gradual development due to his interaction with his natural environment and with his social heritage. The individual born into a particular culture is largely molded by that culture.

FIFTH: Humanism asserts that the nature of the universe depicted by modern science makes unacceptable any supernatural or cosmic guarantees of human values. Obviously, humanism does not deny the possibility of realities as yet undiscovered, but it does insist that the way to determine the existence and value of any and all realities is by means of intelligent inquiry and by the assessment of their relations to human needs. Religion must formulate its hopes and plans in the light of the scientific spirit and method.

SIXTH: We are convinced that the time has passed for theism, deism, modernism, and the several varieties of "new thought".

SEVENTH: Religion consists of those actions, purposes, and experiences which are humanly significant. Nothing human is alien to the religious. It includes labor, art, science, philosophy, love, friendship, recreation–all that is in its degree expressive of intelligently satisfying human living. The distinction between the sacred and the secular can no longer be maintained.

EIGHTH: Religious Humanism considers the complete realization of human personality to be the end of man's life and seeks its development and fulfillment in the here and now. This is the explanation of the humanist's social passion.

NINTH: In the place of the old attitudes involved in worship and prayer the humanist finds his religious emotions expressed in a heightened sense of personal life and in a cooperative effort to promote social well-being.

TENTH: It follows that there will be no uniquely religious emotions and attitudes of the kind hitherto associated with belief in the supernatural.

ELEVENTH: Man will learn to face the crises of life in terms of his knowledge of their naturalness and probability. Reasonable and manly attitudes will be fostered by education and supported by custom. We assume that humanism will take the path of social and mental hygiene and discourage sentimental and unreal hopes and wishful thinking.

TWELFTH: Believing that religion must work increasingly for joy in living, religious humanists aim to foster the creative in man and to encourage achievements that add to the satisfactions of life.

THIRTEENTH: Religious humanism maintains that all associations and institutions exist for the fulfillment of human life. The intelligent evaluation, transformation, control, and direction of such associations and institutions with a view to the enhancement of human life is the purpose and program of humanism. Certainly, religious institutions, their ritualistic forms, ecclesiastical methods, and communal activities must be reconstituted as rapidly as experience allows, in order to function effectively in the modern world.

FOURTEENTH: The humanists are firmly convinced that existing acquisitive and profit-motivated society has shown itself to be inadequate and that a radical change in methods, controls, and motives must be instituted. A socialized and cooperative economic order must be established to the end that the equitable distribution of the means of life be possible. The goal of humanism is a free and universal society in which people voluntarily and intelligently cooperate for the common good. Humanists demand a shared life in a shared world.

FIFTEENTH AND LAST: We assert that humanism will: (a) affirm life rather than deny it; (b) seek to elicit the possibilities of life, not flee from them; and (c) endeavor to establish the conditions of a satis-factory life for all, not merely for the few. By this positive morale and intention humanism will be guided, and from this perspective and alignment the techniques and efforts of humanism will flow.

So, stand the theses of religious humanism. Though we consider the religious forms and ideas of our fathers no longer adequate, the quest for the good life is still the central task for mankind. Man is at last becoming aware that he alone is responsible for the realization of the world of his dreams, that he has within himself the power for its achievement. He must set intelligence and will to the task.

(Signed)

J. A. C. Fagginger Auer — Parkman Professor of Church History and Theology, Harvard University; Professor of Church History, Tufts College.
E. Burdette Backus — Unitarian Minister.
Harry Elmer Barnes — General Editorial Department, ScrippsHoward News-papers.
L. M. Birkhead — The Liberal Center, Kansas City, Missouri.
Raymond B. Bragg— Secretary, Western Unitarian Conference.

Edwin Arthur Burtt — Professor of Philosophy, Sage School of Philosophy, Cornell University.

Ernest Caldecott — Minister, First Unitarian Church, Los Angeles, California.

A. J. Carlson — Professor of Physiology, University of Chicago.

John Dewey — Columbia University.

Albert C. Dieffenbach — Formerly Editor of The Christian Register.

John H. Dietrich — Minister, First Unitarian Society, Minneapolis.

Bernard Fantus — Professor of Therapeutics, College of Medicine, University of Illinois.

William Floyd — Editor of *The Arbitrator*, New York City.

F.H. Hankins — Professor of Economics and Sociology, Smith College.

A. Eustace Haydon — Professor of History of Religions, University of Chicago.

Llewellyn Jones — Literary critic and author.

Robert Morss Lovett — Editor, *The New Republic*; Professor of English, University of Chicago.

Harold P Marley — Minister, The Fellowship of Liberal Religion, Ann Arbor, Michigan.

R. Lester Mondale — Minister, Unitarian Church, Evanston, Illinois.

Charles Francis Potter — Leader and Founder, the First Humanist Society of New York, Inc.

John Herman Randall, Jr.— Department of Philosophy, Columbia University.

Curtis W. Reese — Dean, Abraham Lincoln Center, Chicago.

Oliver L. Reiser — Associate Professor of Philosophy, University of Pittsburgh.

Roy Wood Sellars — Professor of Philosophy, University of Michigan.

Clinton Lee Scott — Minister, Universalist Church, Peoria, Illinois.

Maynard Shipley — President, The Science League of America.

W. Frank Swift — Director, Boston Ethical Society.

V. T. Thayer—Educational Director, Ethical Culture Schools.

Eldred C. Vanderlaan—Leader of the Free Fellowship, Berkeley, California.

Joseph Walker—Attorney, Boston, Massachusetts.

Jacob J. Weinstein—Rabbi; Advisor to Jewish Students, Columbia University.

Frank S. C. Wicks—All Souls Unitarian Church, Indianapolis.

David Rhys Williams—Minister, Unitarian Church, Rochester, New York.

Edwin H. Wilson—Managing Editor, *The New Humanist*, Chicago, Illinois; Minister, Third Unitarian Church, Chicago, Illinois.

The Humanist Manifesto II (1973)

Preface

It is forty years since Humanist Manifesto I (1933) appeared. Events since then make that earlier statement seem far too optimistic. Nazism has shown the depths of brutality of which humanity is capable. Other totalitarian regimes have suppressed human rights without ending poverty. Science has sometimes brought evil as well as good. Recent decades have shown that inhuman wars can be made in the name of peace. The beginnings of police states, even in democratic societies, widespread government espionage, and other abuses of power by military, political, and industrial elites, and the continuance of unyielding racism, all present a different and difficult social outlook. In various societies, the demands of women and minority groups for equal rights effectively challenge our generation.

As we approach the twenty-first century, however, an affirmative and hopeful vision is needed. Faith, commensurate with advancing knowledge, is also necessary. In the choice between despair and hope, humanists respond in this Humanist Manifesto II with a positive declaration for times of uncertainty.

As in 1933, humanists still believe that traditional theism, especially faith in the prayer-hearing God, assumed to live and care for persons, to hear and understand their prayers, and to be able to do something about them, is an unproved and outmoded faith. Salvationism, based on mere affirmation, still appears as harmful, diverting people with false hopes of heaven hereafter. Reasonable minds look to other means for survival.

Those who sign Humanist Manifesto II disclaim that they are setting forth a binding credo; their individual views would be stated in widely varying ways. This statement is, however, reaching for vision in a time that needs direction. It is social analysis in an effort at consensus. New statements should be developed to supersede this, but for today it is our conviction that humanism offers an alternative that can serve present-day needs and guide humankind toward the future.

– Paul Kurtz and Edwin H. Wilson (1973)

The next century can be and should be the humanistic century. Dramatic scientific, technological, and ever-accelerating social and political changes crowd our awareness. We have virtually conquered the planet, explored the moon, overcome the natural limits of travel and communication; we stand at the dawn of a new age, ready to move farther into space and perhaps inhabit other planets. Using technology wisely, we can control our environment, conquer poverty, markedly reduce disease, extend our life-span, significantly modify our behavior, alter the course of human evolution and cultural development, unlock vast new powers, and provide humankind with unparalleled opportunity for achieving an abundant and meaningful life.

The future is, however, filled with dangers. In learning to apply the scientific method to nature and human life, we have opened the door to ecological damage, over-population, dehumanizing institutions, totalitarian repression, and nuclear and bio-chemical disaster. Faced with apocalyptic prophesies and doomsday scenarios, many flee in despair from reason and embrace irrational cults and theologies of withdrawal and retreat.

Traditional moral codes and newer irrational cults both fail to meet the pressing needs of today and tomorrow. False "theologies of hope" and messianic ideologies, substituting new dogmas for old, cannot cope with existing world realities. They separate rather than unite peoples.

Humanity, to survive, requires bold and daring measures. We need to extend the uses of scientific method, not renounce them, to fuse reason with compassion in order to build constructive social and moral values. Confronted by many possible futures, we must decide which to pursue. The ultimate goal should be the fulfillment of the potential for growth in each human personality – not for the favored few, but for all of humankind. Only a shared world and global measures will suffice.

A humanist outlook will tap the creativity of each human being and provide the vision and courage for us to work together. This outlook emphasizes the role human beings can play in their own spheres of action. The decades ahead call for dedicated, clear-minded men and women able to marshal the will, intelligence, and cooperative skills for shaping a desirable future. Humanism can provide the purpose and inspiration that so many seek; it can give personal meaning and significance to human life.

Many kinds of humanism exist in the contemporary world. The varieties and emphases of naturalistic humanism include "scientific," "ethical," "democratic," "religious," and "Marxist" humanism. Free thought, atheism, agnosticism, skepticism, deism, rationalism, ethical culture, and liberal religion all claim to be heir to the humanist tradition. Humanism traces its roots from ancient China, classical Greece and Rome, through the Renaissance and the Enlightenment, to the scientific revolution of the modern world. But views that merely reject theism are not equivalent to humanism. They lack commitment to the positive belief in the possibilities of human progress and to the values central to it. Many within religious groups, believing in the future of humanism, now claim humanist credentials. Humanism is an ethical process through which we all can move, above and beyond the divisive particulars, heroic personalities, dogmatic creeds, and ritual customs of past religions or their mere negation.

We affirm a set of common principles that can serve as a basis for united action – positive principles relevant to the present human condition. They are a design for a secular society on a planetary scale.

For these reasons, we submit this new Humanist Manifesto for the future of humankind; for us, it is a vision of hope, a direction for satisfying survival.

Religion

FIRST: In the best sense, religion may inspire dedication to the highest ethical ideals. The cultivation of moral devotion and creative imagination is an expression of genuine "spiritual" experience and aspiration. We believe, however, that traditional dogmatic or authoritarian religions that place revelation, God, ritual, or creed above human needs and experience do a disservice to the human species. Any account of nature should pass the tests of scientific evidence; in our judgment, the dogmas and myths of traditional religions do not do so. Even at this late date in human history, certain elementary facts based upon the critical use of scientific reason have to be restated. We find insufficient evidence for belief in the existence of a supernatural; it is either meaningless or irrelevant to the question of survival and fulfillment of the human race. As nontheists, we begin with humans not God, nature not deity. Nature may indeed be broader and deeper than we now know; any new discoveries, however, will but enlarge our knowledge of the natural.

Some humanists believe we should reinterpret traditional religions and reinvest them with meanings appropriate to the current situation. Such redefinitions, however, often perpetuate old dependencies and escapisms; they easily become obscurantist, impeding the free use of the intellect. We need, instead, radically new human purposes and goals.

We appreciate the need to preserve the best ethical teachings in the religious traditions of humankind, many of which we share in common. But we reject those features of traditional religious morality that deny humans a full appreciation of their own potentialities and responsibilities. Traditional religions often offer solace to humans, but, as often, they inhibit humans from helping themselves or experiencing their full potentialities. Such institutions, creeds, and rituals often impede the will to serve others. Too often traditional faiths encourage dependence rather than independence, obedience rather than affirmation, fear rather than courage. More recently they have generated concerned social action, with many signs of relevance appearing in the wake of the "God Is Dead" theologies. But we can discover no divine purpose or providence for the human species. While there is much that we do not know, humans are responsible for what we are or will become. No deity will save us; we must save ourselves.

SECOND: Promises of immortal salvation or fear of eternal damnation are both illusory and harmful. They distract humans from present concerns, from self-actualization, and from rectifying social injustices. Modern science discredits such historic concepts as the "ghost in the machine" and the "separable soul." Rather, science affirms that the human species is an emergence from natural evolutionary forces. As far as we know, the total personality is a function of the biological organism transacting in a social and cultural context. There is no credible evidence that life survives the death of the body. We continue to exist in our progeny and in the way that our lives have influenced others in our culture.

Traditional religions are surely not the only obstacles to human progress. Other ideologies also impede human advance. Some forms of political doctrine, for instance, function religiously, reflecting the worst features of orthodoxy and authoritarianism, especially when they sacrifice individuals on the altar of Utopian promises. Purely economic and political viewpoints, whether capitalist or communist, often function as religious and ideological dogma. Although humans undoubtedly need economic and political goals, they also need creative values by which to live.

Ethics

THIRD: We affirm that moral values derive their source from human experience. Ethics is autonomous and situational needing no theological or ideological sanction. Ethics stems from human need and interest. To deny this distorts the whole basis of life. Human life has meaning because we create and develop our futures. Happiness and the creative realization of human needs and desires, individually and in shared enjoyment, are continuous themes of humanism. We strive for the good life, here and now. The goal is to pursue life's enrichment despite debasing forces of vulgarization, commercialization, and dehumanization.

FOURTH: Reason and intelligence are the most effective instruments that humankind possesses. There is no substitute: neither faith nor passion suffices in itself. The controlled use of scientific methods, which have transformed the natural and social sciences since the Renaissance, must be extended further in the solution of human problems. But reason must be tempered by humility, since no group has a monopoly of wisdom or virtue. Nor is there any guarantee that all problems can be solved or all questions answered. Yet critical intelligence, infused by a sense of human caring, is the best method that humanity has for resolving problems. Reason should be balanced with compassion and empathy and the whole person fulfilled. Thus, we are not advocating the use of scientific intelligence independent of or in opposition to emotion, for we believe in the cultivation of feeling and love. As science pushes back the boundary of the known, humankind's sense of wonder is continually renewed, and art, poetry, and music find their places, along with religion and ethics.

The Individual

FIFTH: The preciousness and dignity of the individual person is a central humanist value. Individuals should be encouraged to realize their own creative talents and desires. We reject all religious, ideological, or moral codes that denigrate the individual, suppress freedom, dull intellect, dehumanize personality. We believe in maximum individual autonomy consonant with social responsibility. Although science can account for the causes of behavior, the possibilities of individual freedom of choice exist in human life and should be increased.

SIXTH: In the area of sexuality, we believe that intolerant attitudes, often cultivated by orthodox religions and puritanical cultures, unduly repress sexual conduct. The right to birth control, abortion, and divorce should be recognized. While we do not approve of exploitive, denigrating forms of sexual expression, neither do we wish to prohibit, by law or social sanction, sexual behavior between consenting adults. The many varieties of sexual exploration should not in themselves be considered "evil." Without countenancing mindless permissiveness or unbridled promiscuity, a civilized society should be a tolerant one. Short of harming others or compelling them to do likewise, individuals should be permitted to express their sexual proclivities and pursue their lifestyles as they desire. We wish to cultivate the development of a responsible attitude toward sexuality, in which humans are not exploited as sexual objects, and in which intimacy, sensitivity, respect, and honesty in interpersonal relations are encouraged. Moral education for children and adults is an important way of developing awareness and sexual maturity.

Democratic Society

SEVENTH: To enhance freedom and dignity the individual must experience a full range of civil liberties in all societies. This includes freedom of speech and the press, political democracy, the legal right of opposition to governmental policies, fair judicial process, religious liberty, freedom of association, and artistic, scientific, and cultural freedom. It also includes a recognition of an individual's right to die with dignity, euthanasia, and the right to suicide. We oppose the increasing invasion of privacy, by whatever means, in both totalitarian and democratic societies. We would safeguard, extend, and implement the principles of human freedom evolved from the Magna Carta to the Bill of Rights, the Rights of Man, and the Universal Declaration of Human Rights.

EIGHTH: We are committed to an open and democratic society. We must extend participatory democracy in its true sense to the economy, the school, the family, the workplace, and voluntary associations. Decision-making must be decentralized to include widespread involvement of people at all levels – social, political, and economic. All persons should have a voice in developing the values and goals that determine their lives. Institutions should be responsive to expressed desires and needs. The conditions of work, education, devotion, and play should be humanized. Alienating forces should be modified or eradicated and bureaucratic structures should be held to a minimum. People are more important than decalogues, rules, proscriptions, or regulations.

NINTH: The separation of church and state and the separation of ideology and state are imperatives. The state should encourage maximum freedom for different moral, political, religious, and social values in society. It should not favor any particular religious bodies through the use of public monies, nor espouse a single ideology and function thereby as an instrument of propaganda or oppression, particularly against dissenters.

TENTH: Humane societies should evaluate economic systems not by rhetoric or ideology, but by whether or not they increase economic well-being for all individuals and groups, minimize poverty and hardship, increase the sum of human satisfaction, and enhance the quality of life. Hence the door is open to alternative economic systems. We need to democratize the economy and judge it by its responsiveness to human needs, testing results in terms of the common good.

ELEVENTH: The principle of moral equality must be furthered through elimination of all discrimination based upon race, religion, sex, age, or national origin. This means equality of opportunity and recognition of talent and merit. Individuals should be encouraged to contribute to their own betterment. If unable, then society should provide means to satisfy their basic economic, health, and cultural needs, including, wherever resources make possible, a minimum guaranteed annual income. We are concerned for the welfare of the aged, the infirm, the disadvantaged, and also for the outcasts – the mentally retarded, abandoned, or abused children, the handicapped, prisoners, and addicts – for all who are neglected or ignored by society. Practicing humanists should make it their vocation to humanize personal relations.

We believe in the right to universal education. Everyone has a right to the cultural opportunity to fulfill his or her unique capacities and talents. The schools should foster satisfying and productive living. They should be open at all levels to any and all; the achievement of excellence should be encouraged. Innovative and experimental forms of education are to be welcomed. The energy and idealism of the young deserve to be appreciated and channeled to constructive purposes.

We deplore racial, religious, ethnic, or class antagonisms. Although we believe in cultural diversity and encourage racial and ethnic pride, we reject separations which promote alienation and set people and groups against each other; we envision an integrated community where people have a maximum opportunity for free and voluntary association.

We are critical of sexism or sexual chauvinism – male or female. We believe in equal rights for both women and men to fulfill their unique careers and potentialities as they see fit, free of invidious discrimination.

World Community

TWELFTH: We deplore the division of humankind on nationalistic grounds. We have reached a turning point in human history where the best option is to transcend the limits of national sovereignty and to move toward the building of a world community in which all sectors of the human family can participate. Thus, we look to the development of a system of world law and a world order based upon transnational federal government. This would appreciate cultural pluralism and diversity. It would not exclude pride in national origins and accomplishments nor the handling of regional problems on a regional basis. Human progress, however, can no longer be achieved by focusing on one section of the world, Western or Eastern, developed or underdeveloped. For the first time in human history, no part of humankind can be isolated from any other. Each person's future is in some way linked to all. We thus reaffirm a commitment to the building of world community, at the same time recognizing that this commits us to some hard choices.

THIRTEENTH: This world community must renounce the resort to violence and force as a method of solving international disputes. We believe in the peaceful adjudication of differences by international courts and by the development of the arts of negotiation and compromise. War is obsolete. So is the use of nuclear, biological, and chemical weapons. It is a planetary imperative to reduce the level of military expenditures and turn these savings to peaceful and people-oriented uses.

FOURTEENTH: The world community must engage in cooperative planning concerning the use of rapidly depleting resources. The planet earth must be considered a single ecosystem. Ecological damage, resource depletion, and excessive population growth must be checked by international concord. The cultivation and conservation of nature is a moral value; we should perceive ourselves as integral to the sources of our being in nature. We must free our world from needless pollution and waste, responsibly guarding and creating wealth, both natural and human. Exploitation of natural resources, uncurbed by social conscience, must end.

FIFTEENTH: The problems of economic growth and development can no longer be resolved by one nation alone; they are worldwide in scope. It is the moral obligation of the developed nations to provide – through an international authority that safeguards human rights – massive technical, agricultural, medical, and economic assistance, including birth control techniques, to the developing portions of the globe. World poverty must cease. Hence extreme disproportions in wealth, income, and economic growth should be reduced on a worldwide basis.

SIXTEENTH: Technology is a vital key to human progress and development. We deplore any neo-romantic efforts to condemn indiscriminately all technology and science or to counsel retreat from its further extension and use for the good of humankind. We would resist any moves to censor basic scientific research on moral, political, or social grounds. Technology must, however, be carefully judged by the consequences of its use; harmful and destructive changes should be avoided. We are particularly disturbed when technology and bureaucracy control, manipulate, or modify human beings without their consent. Technological feasibility does not imply social or cultural desirability.

SEVENTEENTH: We must expand communication and transportation across frontiers. Travel restrictions must cease. The world must be open to diverse political, ideological, and moral viewpoints and evolve a worldwide system of television and radio for information and education. We thus call for full international cooperation in culture, science, the arts, and technology across ideological borders. We must learn to live openly together or we shall perish together.

Humanity as a Whole

IN CLOSING: The world cannot wait for a reconciliation of competing political or economic systems to solve its problems. These are the times for men and women of goodwill to further the building of a peaceful and prosperous world. We urge that parochial loyalties and inflexible moral and religious ideologies be transcended. We urge recognition of the common humanity of all people. We further urge the use of reason and compassion to produce the kind of world we want – a world in which peace, prosperity, freedom, and happiness are widely shared. Let us not abandon that vision in despair or cowardice. We are responsible for what we are or will be. Let us work together for a humane world by means commensurate with humane ends. Destructive ideological differences among communism, capitalism, socialism, conservatism, liberalism, and radicalism should be overcome. Let us call for an end to terror and hatred. We will survive and prosper only in a world of shared humane values. We can initiate new directions for humankind; ancient rivalries can be superseded by broad-based cooperative efforts. The commitment to tolerance, understanding, and peaceful negotiation does not necessitate acquiescence to the status quo nor the damming up of dynamic and revolutionary forces. The true revolution is occurring and can continue in countless nonviolent adjustments. But this entails the willingness to step forward onto new and expanding plateaus. At the present juncture of history, commitment to all humankind is the highest commitment of which we are capable; it transcends the narrow allegiances of church, state, party, class, or race in moving toward a wider vision of human potentiality. What more daring a goal for humankind than for each person to become, in ideal as well as practice, a citizen of a world community. It is a classical vision; we can now give it new vitality. Humanism thus interpreted is a moral force that has time on its side. We believe that humankind has the potential, intelligence, goodwill, and cooperative skill to implement this commitment in the decades ahead.

We, the undersigned, while not necessarily endorsing every detail of the above, pledge our general support to Humanist Manifesto II for the future of humankind. These affirmations are not a final credo or dogma but an expression of a living and growing faith. We invite others in all lands to join us in further developing and working for these goals.

Lionel Able, Prof. of English, State Univ. of New York at Buffalo
Khoren Arisian, Board of Leaders, NY Soc. for Ethical Culture

Isaac Asimov, author

George Axtelle, Prof. Emeritus, Southern Illinois Univ.

Archie J. Bahm, Prof. of Philosophy Emeritus, Univ. of N.M.

Pual H. Beattie, Pres., Fellowship of Religious Humanists

Keith Beggs, Exec. Dir., American Humanist Association

Malcolm Bissell, Prof. Emeritus, Univ. of Southern California

H. J. Blackham, Chm., Social Morality Council, Great Britain

Brand Blanshard, Prof. Emeritus, Yale University

Paul Blanshard, author

Joseph L. Blau, Prof. of Religion, Columbia University

Sir Hermann Bondi, Prof. of Math., King's Coll., Univ. of London

Howard Box, Leader, Brooklyn Society for Ethical Culture

Raymond B. Bragg, Minister Emer., Unitarian Ch., Kansas City

Theodore Brameld, Visiting Prof., C.U.N.Y.

Brigid Brophy, author, Great Britain

Lester R. Brown, Senior Fellow, Overseas Development Council

Bette Chambers, Pres., American Humanist Association

John Ciardi, poet

Francis Crick, M.D., Great Britain

Arthur Danto, Prof. of Philosophy, Columbia University

Lucien de Coninck, Prof., University of Gand, Belgium

Miriam Allen deFord, author

Edd Doerr, Americans United for Separation of Church and State

Peter Draper, M.D., Guy's Hospital Medical School, London

Paul Edwards, Prof. of Philosophy, Brooklyn College
Albert Ellis, Exec. Dir., Inst. Adv. Study Rational Psychotherapy
Edward L. Ericson, Board of Leaders, NY Soc. of Ethical Culture
H. J. Eysenck, Prof. of Psychology, Univ. of London
Roy P. Fairfield, Coordinator, Union Graduate School
Herbert Feigl, Prof. Emeritus, Univ. of Minnesota
Raymond Firth, Prof. Emeritus of Anthropology, Univ. of London
Antony Flew, Prof. of Philosophy, The Univ., Reading, England
Kenneth Furness, Exec. Secy., British Humanist Association
Erwin Gaede, Minister, Unitarian Church, Ann Arbor, Mich.
Richard S. Gilbert, Minister, First Unitarian Ch., Rochester, N.Y.
Charles Wesley Grady, Minister, Unit. Univ. Ch., Arlington, Ma.
Maxine Greene, Prof., Teachers College, Columbia University
Thomas C. Greening, Editor, Journal of Humanistic Psychology
Alan F. Guttmacher, Pres., Planned Parenthood Fed. of America
J. Harold Hadley, Min., Unit. Univ. Ch., Pt. Washington, N.Y.
Hector Hawton, Editor, Questions, Great Britain
Eustace Haydon, Prof. Emeritus of History of Religions
James Hemming, Psychologist, Great Britain
Palmer A. Hilty, Adm. Secy., Fellowship of Religious Humanists
Hudson Hoagland, Pres. Emeritus, Worcester Fdn. for Exper. Bio
Robert S. Hoagland, Editor, Religious Humanism
Sidney Hook, Prof. Emeritus of Philosophy, New York University

James F. Hornback, Leader, Ethical Society of St Louis

James M Hutchinson, Minister Emer., First Unit. Ch., Cincinnati

Mordecai M. Kaplan, Rabbi, Fndr. of Jewish Reconstr. Movement

John C. Kidneigh, Prof. of Social Work., Univ. of Minnesota

Lester A. Kirdendall, Prof. Emeritus, Oregon State Univ.

Margaret Knight, Univ. of Aberdeen, Scotland

Jean Kotkin, Exec. Secy., American Ethical Union

Richard Kostelanetz, poet

Paul Kurtz, Editor, The Humanist

Lawrence Lader, Chm., Natl. Assn. for Repeal of Abortion Laws

Edward Lamb, Pres., Lamb Communications, Inc.

Corliss Lamont, Chm., Natl. Emergency Civil Liberties Comm.

Chauncey D. Leake, Prof., Univ. of California, San Francisco

Alfred McC. Lee, Prof. Emeritus, Soc.-Anthropology, C.U.N.Y.

Elizabeth Briant Lee, author

Christopher Macy, Dir., Rationalist Press Assn., Great Britain

Clorinda Margolis, Jefferson Comm. Mental Health Cen., Phila.

Joseph Margolis, Prof. of Philosophy, Temple Univ.

Harold P. Marley, Ret. Unitarian Minister

Floyd W. Matson, Prof. of American Studies, Univ. of Hawaii

Lester Mondale, former Pres., Fellowship of Religious Humanists

Lloyd Morain, Pres., Illinois Gas Company

Mary Morain, Editorial Bd., Intl. Soc. of General Semantics

Charles Morris, Prof. Emeritus, Univ. of Florida

Henry Morgentaler, M.D., Past Pres., Humanist Assn. of Canada

Mary Mothersill, Prof. of Philosophy, Bernard College

Jerome Nathanson, Chm. Bd. of Leaders, NY Soc. Ethical Culture

Billy Joe Nichols, Minister, Richardson Unitarian Church, Texas

Kai Nielsen, Prof. of Philosophy, Univ. of Calgary, Canada

P. H. Nowell-Smith, Prof. of Philosophy, York Univ., Canada

Chaim Perelman, Prof. of Philosophy, Univ. of Brussels, Belgium

James W. Prescott, Natl, Inst. of Child Health and Human Dev.

Harold J. Quigley, Leader, Ethical Humanist Society of Chicago

Howard Radest, Prof. of Philosophy, Ramapo College

John Herman Randall, Jr., Prof. Emeritus, Columbia Univ.

Oliver L. Reiser, Prof. Emeritus, Univ. of Pittsburgh

Robert G. Risk, Pres., Leadville Corp.

Lord Ritchie-Calder, formerly Univ. of Edinburgh, Scotland

B. T. Rocca, Jr., Consultant, Intl. Trade and Commodities

Andre H. Sakharov, Academy of Sciences, Moscow, U.S.S.R.

Sidney H. Scheuer, Chm., Natl, Comm. for an Effective Congress

Herbert W. Schneider, Prof. Emeritus, Claremont Grad. School

Clinton Lee Scott, Universalist Minister, St Petersburgh, Fla.

Roy Wood Sellars, Prof. Emeritus, Univ. of Michigan

A. B. Shah, Pres., Indian Secular Society

B. F. Skinner, Prof. of Psychology, Harvard Univ.

Kenneth J. Smith, Leader, Philadelphia Ethical Society

Matthew Ies Spetter, Chm., Dept. Ethics, Ethical Culture Schools

Mark Starr, Chm., Esperanto Info. Center

Svetozar Stojanovic, Prof. Philosophy, Univ. Belgrade, Yugoslavia

Harold Taylor, Project Director, World University Student Project

V. T. Thayer, author

Herbert A. Tonne, Ed. Board, Journal of Business Education

Jack Tourin, Pres., American Ethical Union

E. C. Vanderlaan, lecturer

J. P. van Praag, Chm., Intl. Humanist and Ethical Union, Utrecht

Maurice B. Visscher, M.D., Prof. Emeritus, Univ. of Minnesota

Goodwin Watson, Assn. Coordinator, Union Graduate School

Gerald Wendt, author

Henry N. Wieman, Prof. Emeritus, Univ. of Chicago

Sherwin Wine, Rabbi, Soc. for Humanistic Judaism

Edwin H. Wilson, Ex. Dir. Emeritus, American Humanist Assn.

Bertram D. Wolfe, Hoover Institution

Alexander S. Yesenin-Volpin, mathematician

Marvin Zimmerman, Prof. of Philosophy, State Univ. NY at Bflo.

The Humanist Manifesto III (2003)

Humanism is a progressive philosophy of life that, without super-naturalism, affirms our ability and responsibility to lead ethical lives of personal fulfillment that aspire to the greater good of humanity.

The life stance of Humanism—guided by reason, inspired by compassion, and informed by experience—encourages us to live life well and fully. It evolved through the ages and continues to develop through the efforts of thoughtful people who recognize that values and ideals, however carefully wrought, are subject to change as our knowledge and understandings advance.

This document is part of an ongoing effort to manifest in clear and positive terms the conceptual boundaries of Humanism, not what we must believe but a consensus of what we do believe. It is in this sense that we affirm the following:

Knowledge of the world is derived by observation, experimentation, and rational analysis. Humanists find that science is the best method for determining this knowledge as well as for solving problems and developing beneficial technologies. We also recognize the value of new departures in thought, the arts, and inner experience—each subject to analysis by critical intelligence.

Humans are an integral part of nature, the result of unguided evolutionary change. Humanists recognize nature as self-existing. We accept our life as all and enough, distinguishing things as they are from things as we might wish or imagine them to be. We welcome the challenges of the future, and are drawn to and undaunted by the yet to be known.

Ethical values are derived from human need and interest as tested by experience. Humanists ground values in human welfare shaped by human circumstances, interests, and concerns and extended to the global ecosystem and beyond. We are committed to treating each person as having inherent worth and dignity, and to making informed choices in a context of freedom consonant with responsibility.

Life's fulfillment emerges from individual participation in the service of humane ideals. We aim for our fullest possible development and animate our lives with a deep sense of purpose, finding wonder and awe in the joys and beauties of human existence, its challenges and tragedies, and even in the inevitability and finality of death. Humanists rely on the rich heritage of human culture and the life stance of Humanism to provide comfort in times of want and encouragement in times of plenty.

Humans are social by nature and find meaning in relationships. Humanists long for and strive toward a world of mutual care and concern, free of cruelty and its consequences, where differences are resolved co-operatively without resorting to violence. The joining of individuality with interdependence enriches our lives, encourages us to enrich the lives of others, and inspires hope of attaining peace, justice, and opportunity for all.

Working to benefit society maximizes individual happiness. Progressive cultures have worked to free humanity from the brutalities of mere survival and to reduce suffering, improve society, and develop global community. We seek to minimize the inequities of circumstance and ability, and we support a just distribution of nature's resources and the fruits of human effort so that as many as possible can enjoy a good life.

Humanists are concerned for the well being of all, are committed to diversity, and respect those of differing yet humane views. We work to uphold the equal enjoyment of human rights and civil liberties in an open, secular society and maintain it is a civic duty to participate in the democratic process and a planetary duty to protect nature's integrity, diversity, and beauty in a secure, sustainable manner.

Thus, engaged in the flow of life, we aspire to this vision with the informed conviction that humanity has the ability to progress toward its highest ideals. The responsibility for our lives and the kind of world in which we live is ours and ours alone.

Further Learning

Learning More About Humanism and Humanist Varieties

Books

Ericson, Edward. *The Humanist Way: An Introduction to Ethical Humanist Religion*

Halstead, John. *Godless Paganism*

Kitcher, Philip. *Life After Faith: The Case for Secular Humanism*

Olds, Mason. *Religious Humanism in America*

Wine, Sherwin. *Judaism Beyond God*

Websites

American Ethical Union
http://aeu.org/

American Humanist Association
www.americanhumanist.org

Humanists UK (formerly the British Humanist Association)
https://humanism.org.uk/

Center for Inquiry
http://www.centerforinquiry.net/

The Humanist Society
http://thehumanistsociety.org/

Humanistic Paganism
https://humanisticpaganism.com/

International Humanist and Ethical Union
http://iheu.org/

Spiritualist Naturalist Society

http://spiritualnaturalistsociety.org/

The Unitarian Universalist Humanist Association

http://huumanists.org/

Learning More About Humanist History and Philosophy

Books

Epstein, Greg. *Good Without God*

Gaylor, A.C. *Women Without Superstition*

Jacoby, Susan. *Freethinkers*

Lamont, Corliss. *The Philosophy of Humanism*

Larue, Gerald. *Freethought Across the Centuries*

Websites

Corliss Lamont

http://www.corliss-lamont.org/

Humanist Manifesto III

http://americanhumanist.org/humanism/humanist_manifesto_iii

The Humanist Philosophy in Perspective - Frederick Edwords

http://infidels.org/library/modern/fred_edwords/perspective.html

Kochhar Online Humanist Education

http://cohe.humanistinstitute.org/

Notes

1. Our History. The Humanist Society. http://thehumanistsociety. org/about/history/.

2. Inspired in part by, Edwords, Fred. *What Is Humanism?* American Humanist Association, 2008. http://americanhumanist.org/humanism/what_is_humanism.

3. Speckhardt, Roy. *When 'Humanist' Is a Cop-out (And When It Isn't).* The Huffington Post. April 06, 2016. http://www.huffingtonpost. com/roy-speckhardt/when-humanist-is-a-cop-ou_b_9625976. html.

4. *Exploring the Idea of humanism.* American Humanist Association. http://americanhumanist.org/humanism.

5. Edwords, Fred. E-mail message to author. June 7, 2016.

6. Humanist Society Guidelines. The Humanist Society. http://the-humanistsociety.org/about/guidelines/.

7. http://iheu.org/about/about-iheu/

8. "Avalon Project - Blackstone's Commentaries on the Laws of England - Book the First : Chapter the Fifteenth : Of Husband and Wife." Avalon Project - Blackstone's Commentaries on the Laws of England - Book the First : Chapter the Fifteenth : Of Husband and Wife. 2008. http://avalon.law.yale.edu/18th_century/blackstone_bk1ch15.asp.

9. Alain de Botton, *Status Anxiety* (Toronto: Penguin Group Canada, 2005), 223.

10. "Secularism to Be Represented at Va. University Founder's Day Breakfast Tomorrow - Freedom from Religion Foundation." Secularism to Be Represented at Va. University Founder's Day Breakfast Tomorrow - Freedom from Religion Foundation. September 17, 2015. Accessed July 12, 2016. http://ffrf.org/news/news-releases/item/24044-nonbelief-to-be-represented-at-friday-s-va-university-founder-s-day-breakfast.

11. "Endorsements Available." The Humanist Society http://thehumanistsociety.org/apply/endorsements/.

Picture credits

Page 35:	David Spencer
Page 45:	Min Enterprises Photography LLC
Page 46:	Milestones Secular Rites
Page 48:	Milestones Secular Rites
Page 50:	Amy Bowman
Page 56:	Milestones Secular Rites
Page 64:	James Bass Photography
Page 66:	InSight Foto Inc
Page 68:	Milestones Secular Rites
Page 71:	Alex Maxwell
Page 73:	Alex Maxwell
Page 79:	Milestones Secular Rites
Page 81:	Milestones Secular Rites
Page 85:	Milestones Secular Rites
Page 86:	Milestones Secular Rites
Page 87:	David Spencer
Page 89:	Milestones Secular Rites
Page 89:	Milestones Secular Rites
Page 90:	Milestones Secular Rites
Page 94:	Min Enterprises Photography LLC

Page 154:   Lijuan Guo | Dreamstime
Page 162:   Korn Vitthayanukarun | Dreamstime
Page 203:   Jennifer and Tim Bailey, Celebrating Times of Change, LLC
Page 213:   Courtesy of Victoria Gipson
Page 215:   Courtesy of Victoria Gipson
Page 223:   Milestones Secular Rites

CPSIA information can be obtained
at www.ICGtesting.com
Printed in the USA
BVOW05s0248040118
504413BV00004B/6/P